The Scope of Biblical Prophecy:
A General Survey

Donald R. Whitchard

Parson's Porch Books

The Scope of Biblical Prophecy: A General Survey
ISBN: Softcover 978-1-955581-61-5
Copyright © 2022 by Donald Whitchard

Parson's Porch Books is an imprint of Parson's Porch *&* Company (PP*&*C) in Cleveland, Tennessee. PP*&*C is an innovative organization which raises money by publishing books of noted authors, representing all genres. Its face and voice is **David Russell Tullock** (dtullock@parsonsporch. com).

Parson's Porch *&* Company *turns books into bread & milk* by sharing its profits with the poor.

www. parsonsporch. com

The Scope of Biblical Prophecy:

A General Survey

Contents

Introduction

Before we enter the study of biblical prophecy and its characteristics, theology, evidence, and interpretation, I would like the reader to know something about myself. I am an ordained minister of the Southern Baptist Convention. I have been steeped since my childhood in the fact that the Scriptures we possess are without error and changes lives when they are studied along with the presentation of those concepts and truths God has chosen to reveal to us. I believe that God primarily speaks to us from Scripture and that there no further revelation is needed. This is not to say that God cannot impress upon us to pray for a lost person, loved one, or friend. He gives us wisdom and grace through prayer, godly counsel, sound teaching, and the preaching of the Word and its application to one's heart. My background, theological training, and years of studying Scripture has had me to conclude that much of what passes for the Christian faith now seems to be based upon emotional experiences and false doctrines.

I have been a Christian for over forty years, having been led to Christ by a gospel program on TV and receiving a call to full-time ministry, namely that of evangelism and teaching. I have served as a pastor, hospital chaplain, high school and bible college teacher, and time as an interim pastor in small churches in Louisiana and Oklahoma where I now reside. My theological and doctrinal beliefs and convictions have grown and matured over the years, and I have spent many hours in studying topics such as the deity of Christ, the sovereignty of God, the ministry of the Holy Spirit, the mission of the church, spiritual warfare, and prophecy. I have been interested in prophecy from my earliest days as a believer and I have watched events unfold in recent years that have tended to convince me that the Lord Jesus Christ is coming soon.

However, a fixation on biblical prophecy should not be our only area of interest. It should never serve as the exclusive doctrine to test a person's convictions or orthodoxy. What people believe about issues like the timing of the rapture is not a salvation issue. It is in our best interest to examine all valid points of view which will be presented in the chapters to come. There will be a look into selected Scriptures for analysis and interpretive study and how they relate to orthodox belief. The study of prophecy is fascinating and informative, but it does no good for you if you don't have a personal relationship with the Lord Jesus Christ, who is the Center of all prophecy, both in the Old and New Testaments.

If you are not sure where you stand before the LORD or express a genuine interest and curiosity about the forth coming material and yet know that you are not right with God, then let's settle that issue now. There are some vital things you need to know. First, just because you think you are a "good" person does not mean that God is going to allow you to get into His heaven. Without the LORD as a foundation for moral and ethical behavior, then "good" is whatever you make of it. You can say that society establishes the foundation of "good" behavior, but what about the moral and ethical standard of, say, Nazi Germany or Communist Russia a generation ago? They thought that what they were doing was perfectly acceptable and legal in their own eyes. This kind of thought came at a high level of bloodshed and carnage as a result of revolutions, wars, and persecution of people like the Jews and believers in Christ. Millions lie in graves because of ungodly standards that were based on prejudice and atheism.

Passages of Scripture such as Romans 1:18-32 and 3:10-18 show us ourselves as to who we truly are, and it is not flattering. Our bad behavior started in Eden, when the federal head of humanity, Adam, rebelled against the holiness of God and His guidance (Genesis 3:6-19). We became enemies of God and continued to reject and renounce Him throughout history. His chosen people, Israel, did not fare much better. Their story is a mixture of devotion and rank apostasy towards God. No one, in the shape they are in, can ever save themselves and be right before a holy and majestic God. In our rebellious state, we deserve punishment in hell (Matthew 25:41; Revelation 20:11-15). This is not pleasant, but I hope that what I have written will cause you to think seriously about your eternal destiny.

There is no way we can be justified before God in our present condition. God Himself had to intervene if the situation were to get any better. Even though we are God's enemies, He has not given up on us and does love us. He loves us so much that He sent His only begotten Son, the Lord Jesus Christ, to come to earth and live as one of us, fully human and fully God. He lived a sinless life and took it upon Himself the task of paying for our sins as the perfect sacrifice for our sins (John 3:16; Romans 5:6-11.8:31-39; Ephesians 2:4-5; Hebrews 9:28; 1 Peter 2:24, and 1 John 3:5). He went through terrible torture and humiliation, dying on a cruel cross as the final, irreversible and total payment for our iniquities. He rose again from the dead after three days (Luke 24:1-12), appeared to His disciples and the apostle Paul affirmed that over five hundred brethren personally saw Him (1 Corinthians 15: 1-9). He ascended to heaven (Acts 1:9-11), where He resides with God the Father and will, according to His promise, return to this world to rid it of sin forever, to rule and reign as King in the new heaven and the new earth (Revelation, Chapters. 21 and 22).

If what I have written makes sense thus far and you believe it, then God's Holy Spirit is gently directing you to Him and is inviting you to receive Jesus Christ as Lord and Savior. Do not put this off. You have no guarantee of tomorrow (2 Corinthians 6:2; James 4: 13-14). If you are ready to ask Jesus to be your Lord and Savior, then talk to Him in your own words. If you are not sure how to do it, then use this prayer as a guide:

"Dear God, I realize that I've rebelled against you. I am a sinner and cannot save myself. I do not want to be your enemy. I deserve judgment, but I ask for mercy from you. I ask that Jesus Christ save me from my sins and come into my life right now. I confess Him as Lord. I believe that He died for me, rose again, and that I can live with Him forever. I ask that your Holy Spirit guide and teach me. I will live for you from this day forward. Thank You, In Jesus' name, Amen."

If you have been away from the LORD, then ask Him to forgive you and renew your devotion to Him. He is willing to receive you with open arms. I just want to say, "Welcome to the family of God!" to the new believer and "Welcome back home" to those who have strayed. The Good Shepherd has sought out and brought back His lost lamb into the fold. Now, you need to do a few things as part of your new life with Jesus Christ.

Get a good study Bible in a translation that you can read and understand such as the New American Standard, or a favorite of many, the King James Version. Read and study it daily. If you are not sure where to begin, I suggest starting in the Gospel of Luke and then the book of Acts to get a good picture of Jesus' work and the early church. Find a good, Bible teaching and believing church. Be faithful to the congregation and the pastor (Hebrews 10:25). Get in a Bible study group at your church and grow spiritually. Tell someone about the decision you have just made. This is too good to keep to yourself (Mark 16:15; Matthew 28:18-20). We are to spread the Good News to everyone in whom we come into contact. Not everybody will listen, but you leave the results to the Holy Spirit. He does the job of opening spiritual eyes. The condition of your soul is something I cannot take for granted. I want you to fall in love with Jesus and learn everything you can about Him, including sound teaching on the issue of biblical prophecy.

Chapter 1
Establishing Terms and Characteristics

There is a great deal of worry, concern, and confusion concerning the direction this nation and the world is taking, leading many people to believe that it will all lead to a frightening conclusion. The doomsday clock keeps inching closer to midnight. Reports of mass animal deaths, unusual weather patterns, the rise of earthquakes and natural disasters, and the moral compass obviously broken by a society that rejects the principles and dictates of Almighty God all point to the fact that we can't go on like this much longer and that something is fixing to happen and not for the better in many opinions. Out of despair and hopelessness, suicide rates are on the rise and people are turning to anything that will give them some semblance of peace.

It doesn't take a lot of effort to check sources on the internet and somewhat reliable alternate news agencies to see that even Christians, or at least those who claim to be believers, are adopting behaviors and attitudes that do not represent a biblical worldview. There is apparently no fear of God in the evangelical world. The principles found in Proverbs 1: 7 seem to fall upon the ears of deliberately ignorant and spiritually compromised so- called "people of faith". This is rather harsh, but when you have reports of Christians divorcing at the same rate as the world, denying the Virgin Birth, advocating doctrines and teachings based on experiences and feelings instead of upon the Word of God, believing Jesus could have sinned, and some proclaiming that there is more than one way to get to heaven, there is definitely trouble.

Enter the prophet, a man chosen by God Himself not just to proclaim what will happen in history, but to call the people to repent. There have been voices throughout biblical history that declared that God's word would be the standard by which a person and nation is supposed to behave. He was called of God to present those events that will happen (prophecy) and to warn the people of judgment for sinful behavior. It was not a job for the timid or brash.

There were consequences for false prophecies and prophets (Deuteronomy 18: 20-22) and the people were not to consult mediums or sorcerers in order to know the future (Leviticus 19: 26; Deuteronomy 18: 9-14). That law has largely fallen on deaf ears in modern times. What was forbidden by God in the days of ancient Israel concerning this wickedness is still applicable today.

For example, statistics from the American Federation of Certified Psychics and Mediums state that a "successful" psychic can earn up to $5,000,000 per year, while "reasonably successful" psychics earn $500,000 a year, and the "average" one can earn anywhere from $75,000 to $150,000 per year. (1) One supposes that those who are successful, as defined by the world, or average are the ones who present alleged "predictions" for the tabloid newspaper each year, of which none come true. Answers.yahoo.com report that Americans spend approximately $300 million per year on "psychic hotlines", calling mediums to get guidance on what to do with their lives (2). There are numerous psychic websites available on the internet, each offering, for a price, advice and counsel that is at best, lucky guesses and generalities. This is clearly a satanic counterfeit to the genuine words from God written on order to encourage and warn people.

So, what is true prophecy? It is nothing like what so-called "psychics" and necromancers can divulge. Webster's 1828 Dictionary defines prophecy as "a foretelling prediction; a declaration of something to come. No being but God or some person informed by Him can utter such" (3) True prophecy comes from the Scriptures, and nowhere else. Some applicable quotes are worth mentioning. Here are some from brainyquote.com (4)

"Only Jesus has prophecies made hundreds of years in advance made literally true. Only He did miracles, only His immediate followers claimed He died and rose from the dead, so in comparison, He comes out superior to other great religious leaders." –Norman Geisler

"Prophecy is an intercept from the mind of an all-knowing and all-seeing and all-powerful God." – Joel Rosenberg

"I've read the last page of the Bible. It's going to turn out all right." – Billy Graham (1918-2018)

"You have to take Bible prophecy literally, just like everything else in the Bible." – Tim LaHaye

As mentioned in the introduction, prophecy does no good if you or someone you know does not have a personal relationship with Jesus Christ.

Here is solid advice from a preacher of the previous century. It is from christianquotes.com (5):

"I know that some are always studying the meaning of the fourth toe of the right foot of some beast in prophecy and have never used either foot to go and bring men to Christ. I do not know who the 666 in Revelation is, but I know the world is sick, sick, sick, and the best way to speed the Lord's return is to win more souls for Him." – Vance.

Prophecy is fascinating, but like what has been stated, it is not everything in the believer's life. However, it is important to know if only for the fact that it gets us excited about the conclusion and that is the return of Jesus Christ. Dr. Mark Hitchcock, in his book creatively entitled The End (6), presents ten reasons as to why Bible prophecy is so encouraging:

1) Much of the Bible is prophetic in nature. Some facts to consider are that there are 31,124 verses in the Bible, with 6,641 out of 23,210 verses of the Old Testament being prophetic. 28.5 % of the Old Testament is prophecy. In the New Testament there are 578 predictions, and the number of New Testament verse that deal with the prophetic are 1,711 out of 7,914. 21.5% of the New Testament is prophetic. 27% of the Bible deals with prophecy. Other facts to consider are that of the 333 verses concerning Jesus Christ, only 109 were fulfilled by His first coming, which means that 224 are yet to be fulfilled! Dr. Hitchcock writes that there are over three hundred references to the Lord's coming in the 260 chapters of the New Testament, which breaks down to 1 in 30 verses. 23 of the 27 books of the New Testament mentions the Lord's coming, and Jesus referred to His Second Coming at least 21 times. 1,527 Old Testament verses refer to the Second Coming. For every time the Bible mentions the first coming, the Second Coming is mentioned 8 times. These are fascinating numbers to consider and give evidence that what we have is God's inerrant word.

2) A special blessing is promised to those who study prophecy and pay attention to what it says (Revelation 1: 3). Revelation is the only book that contains this specific and unique promise (1:3; 14:13; 16:15; 19:9; 20:6 and 22: 7, 14).

3) The subject of prophecy is Jesus Christ. It begins and ends in the person and work of our Lord and Savior. Below are promises and fulfilled prophetic declarations. Here are examples of all that Jesus accomplished:

a. The Seed of the woman, who would crush Satan's head (Genesis 3:15).

b. Shiloh, as predicted by Jacob, meaning royalty would come from the line of Judah (Genesis 49:10)

c. The Passover Lamb (Exodus 12; John 1:29)

d. The star from Jacob (Numbers 24: 17)

e. The great High Priest (Psalm 110)

f. The Prophet (Deuteronomy 18:18)

g. The King (2 Samuel 7: Luke 1: 32 -33)

h. He who is Wonderful, Counselor, the Mighty God, Everlasting Father, and the Prince of Peace (Isaiah 9:6).

I. The Servant (Isaiah 53: 2) and a Man of Sorrows (v. 3)

J. The Smiting Stone (Daniel 2: 31-35) and the Son of Man (Daniel 7:13) as well as the Anointed One (Daniel 9:25-26)

k. The Son who will rule the world (Psalm 2)

l. The Resurrection and the Life (John 11: 25-27)

m. The glorified, risen Savior (Revelation 1)

o. The Lord of the church (Revelation 2 and 3)

p. The Lamb of God (Revelation 5:6)

q. The Judge of the nations (Revelation, Chapters 6-11)

r. The Coming King (Revelation 19)

s. The Lord of heaven and earth (Revelation 20-22)

Prophecy gives us a proper perspective in life. People today tend to mentally and spiritually wander, without any foreseen purpose or direction, which is a point that I made earlier. Bible prophecy gives us meaning and tells us that this life is not all there is. It tells us the end of the story. It is our guidance system and tells us where we are going, giving meaning, perspective, purpose, and helps us embrace hope in life. Bible prophecy is the vehicle God has given to us to reveal His plan for history and provides a goal in our thinking about life and its purpose.

Prophecy helps us understand the whole Bible. Understanding God's absolute, solid plans allows us to be confident in our understanding of the absolute truth of the Bible from Genesis to Revelation. It gives us God's plan for His people, the Jews, plans for the Gentile nations, and the church of Jesus Christ. Prophecy is a tool for evangelism. Many people have been saved from hell because somebody told them what the Scriptures say about the future. Even non-believers are interested in prophecy. Teaching them about events found in Scripture is a way to share your faith. There are several full-time evangelists who specialize in prophecy.

Prophecy helps people steer away from heretical teaching. False teachers have attacked the teachings and ministry of the Lord Jesus since the first century. Almost every book in the New Testament contains references concerning this issue. The teachings of Jesus, Paul, and the apostles in New Testament books such as 2 Corinthians, Galatians, Philippians, 1 and 2 Timothy, Titus , 2 Peter and Jude warn us about deception from false teachers.

Prophecy motivates us to live godly lives. The doctrines of the faith should always guide us in making a practical difference in how we live each day. God intends for prophecy to change our attitudes and actions so they will be more in line with His words and character. God gave us prophecy to change our hearts and not to simply fill our heads with knowledge.

Prophecy reveals the sovereignty of God over time and history. God rules sovereignly over His world. He is present everywhere, knows all things and possesses all power. He has the power to fulfill all prophecies and challenges any pretenders to His position of supremacy in the universe. Only He can accurately predict the future (Isaiah 41: 21-24; 42:9; 44:6-8; 46: 8-11; Daniel 2:20-22). This is a great comfort and solace and an encouragement to know that God has His hands on every area of your life if you belong to Him in Christ.

Prophecy proves the truth of God's word. The Bible contains 1,000 prophecies of which 500 have been fulfilled. The Bible has a track record of 100% accuracy. Examples include the prediction of Cyrus as an agent of liberation for the exiled Jews (Isaiah 44: 28; 45: 1, 2-6), made 160 years before Cyrus was born, The Scriptures mention four great world empires

(Daniel 2, 7) and the 70-year captivity of the Jews in Babylon (Jeremiah 25; 10 -11; 29:10)

Now we come to the office and call of a prophet. In his book The Heart of Hebrew History (7), Dr. H.I. Hester states that the prophets were powerful leaders of religious, social, and even political life in Old Testament history. They were men with a message from God. The very name "prophet" is a significant one. He goes on to say that there are three Hebrew words that are translated "prophets".

Ro'eh/chozeh – these words were used eleven and twenty-two times in Scripture. These two words mean "to see". It referred to a man of vision, called a "seer". This term was used by Saul and his servant when their father's donkeys were lost (1 Samuel 9: 6-11). References to "seers" are found in passages such as 2 Samuel 15:27; 24:11. 1 Chronicles 25:5, 26, 29; 2 Chronicles 16: 7, 19:2, and 35:15. The "seer" was implied that he had the ability to obtain a knowledge of spiritual realities not available to others.

Nabi – this term is used some 300 times. It means "to announce" or to "bubble up". It also means "one who speaks for someone else". It represents the prophet as a speaker. He is one who has received in a special manner a vital message and one who must declare and speak that message (1 Kings 18:21; Isaiah 7:14; 9:6; 11:1; 53; Jeremiah 31 :31 -34; Ezekiel 18: 19-24; Daniel 2:24 -45; 9:27)

Propheteou (Gk.) – A New Testament term meaning "one who brings God's word to his fellow man; one who speaks for God; the word and will of God". The tasks of a man of God, whether he be called a "seer" or "propheteou", was numerous. Over the years of personal study concerning the work and world of the prophets, distinct characteristics have emerged and taken shape concerning them:

The prophet taught the people revelation from God. Whatever the prophet said had to be a direct word from the LORD. There was no room for error or half-truths. There was a penalty for false prophecies which ended in death for the one who practiced them (Deuteronomy 18: 20 -22). This should be a word of warning for anyone who claims to have a "direct revelation" from God that comes from their own experience and emotions that are not based upon Scripture. Rebuke and avoid them if what they proclaim does NOT line up with the Word of God! The Holy Spirit has given us everything the LORD has to say in the Scriptures. The biblical prophetic office is no longer needed today. Today, it is the preacher's duty to warn the people based on the Word about the penalty for ungodly behavior and how to get right with God through Jesus Christ. There are teachers of prophecy today who present lessons from the Bible exclusively and who are used to show their listeners that Jesus is coming back soon.

The prophets taught the people how to worship God. In the first five books of Scripture, the Torah, there is the story of creation, the beginning of the Jewish people, the Divine liberation of Israel from the hands of the Egyptians, and a detailed plan on the building of the Tabernacle, Israel's meeting place with God (Exodus 26-27). God taught His people how to approach and worship Him. Moses the Lawgiver was also considered to be a prophet (Deuteronomy 18:18) and led the people to venerate God and praise Him. David, like Moses, was also seen as one of God's prophets (Psalm 22: 1-18; 110: 1-7). He composed most of the Psalms and throughout the Old Testament, God's messengers stressed the need to glorify God in all things that are pleasing to Him.

The prophets warned the people about the penalties for disobeying God. Other than presenting oracles of future events, there was a prime motivator for God's men, both in the Old and New Testaments. Here is where the word *Nabi* comes into focus. We read of prophets like Samuel, who warned the people about what would happen if they rejected God as ruler and wanted an earthly king (1 Samuel 8), of Elijah who told the people of Israel to make up their minds about who to serve (1 Kings 18: 21). We can also look at the works of the Major Prophets (Isaiah, Jeremiah, Ezekiel, Daniel) and who are called the Minor Prophets (Hosea, Joel, Amos, Obadiah, Jonah, Micah, Nahum, Habakkuk, Zephaniah, Haggai, Zechariah, Malachi) and see that their work centered on calling the people of Israel to come back to God and honor Him, lest they face the terrible consequences.

The prophets warned about God's judgment, the crux of prophetic ministry. The Old Testament contains numerous proclamations of judgment, such as when the prophet Elijah predicted a gruesome ending for the reign of wicked King Ahab for the murder of Naboth (1 Kings 21: 19 -24) concerning his vineyard. God will never allow sin to go unpunished and the prophets declared this to be so. There is a coming judgment upon all peoples, not just rulers and nations. This is an absolute truth that should frighten anyone who mocks God. Nothing will be ignored or looked over and dismissed. Passages of judgment include Isaiah 40:29; Jeremiah 17:10; 32:19; 34:17, Ezekiel 18: 20, 30; Amos 8:7; Matthew 16:27; Romans 2:6; 2

Corinthians 5:10; Revelation 2: 23; 20:12, and 22:12. Let this be a warning to the unsaved and a word of examination to the child of God.

The prophets also proclaimed the coming of a Messiah to save the people of Israel. The concept of a Messiah ("anointed one") in the Scriptures appears after the fall of man in Eden. Sin had entered the world because of disobedience brought on by the tempting words of Satan, who came to Eve in the form of a serpent and deceived her, and in turn brought about Adam's downfall. God cursed the serpent and then gave to the fallen couple a promise found in Genesis 3:15, promising a Redeemer who would defeat the wiles of the serpent once and for all. The Old Testament beams with messianic promises. A few of these promises have been presented earlier in this chapter. Attention will be given to what is the most profound of messianic prophecies, namely Isaiah 52: 13-15 and Chapter 53.

The prophet anointed and rebuked kings, first initiated by the anointing of Saul (1 Samuel 9: 27; 10:1) by the prophet Samuel, who later anointed David (1 Samuel 16: 13) after Saul proved to be a failure due to pride and disobedience. With the rise and promotion of apostasy in the Northern Kingdom of Israel, the prophet Elijah was commissioned by God to anoint new kings over Syria and Israel (1 Kings 19:15-17). Earlier, in 2 Samuel 12, the prophet Nathan confronted David over his adulterous relationship with Bathsheba and the murder of her husband, the faithful soldier Uriah. Jesus, in His role as a prophetic voice, denounced the hypocrisy of the Pharisees, who were the spiritual rulers of Israel (Matthew 23), and His forerunner, John the Baptist, warned people to flee from the wrath to come (Matthew 3: 7-12; Luke 3:7-9). This was not a popular work, but God must be honored. The prophet's messages were not often welcome by the populace. Nobody likes to be confronted with their sins, but the Sovereign Lord God sees everything going on and the prophet affirmed it. The idea of a judgment for sin was abhorrent to the apostate Israelites and the fact that a man of God would point that out was a source of both national and personal conflict.

The prophets proclaimed God's righteousness and mercy for repentance. Examples of this include 2 Chronicles 7: 14; Nehemiah 1: 9; Jeremiah 3: 2; 31: 9, and Ezekiel 18: 21. God did not want sin to go on, but for people and nations to repent of it and be given new chances and hope, with a restoration of a relationship between God and His people. The following verses demonstrate the great mercy of God, such as Psalm 18:50; 25:6: 85: 3; 103:11; 106:8; Jeremiah 3: 5; 51:5; Ezekiel 18: 23; Hosea 11:9; Luke 1:73;

7:42; Romans 9: 15-18, and 1 Timothy 1:16. For this, we should always be grateful.

The prophets sought solitude with God, a time to be alone and revere Him. Our Lord Jesus sought solitude with the Father and spent time in prayer with Him. Those times were apparent when He prayed in the Garden of Gethsemane, concerning the mission He was to undertake on our behalf. Elijah, the Old Testament prophet who, in fear for his life, was comforted by the presence of God and counseled not to be afraid. God had more work for him to do. They were persecuted for bringing the word of God. God's followers were constantly subjected to ridicule and scorn. The Scriptures describe numerous sufferings and hardships for God's messengers. Christ, as Prophet, Priest, and King was subject to the most brutal of persecutions by being nailed to a cross for the sins of the people.

It was not in vain, for it brought about the salvation of His people and more. Persecutions are promised for God's messengers and people (2 Timothy 3:12), but we are also the heirs of a new heaven and a new earth and eternal fellowship with the LORD. C. Hassel Bullock, in his book An Introduction to the Old Testament Prophetic Books (8), states on pages 14 and 15 that these prophets can be placed into three periods of history. First, there was the *Neo-Assyrian* period, whose attention fell upon the circumstances leading up to and the conditions following the fall of the Northern Kingdom in 722 B.C. The prophets of this period are Amos, Hosea, Micah, and Isaiah. They saw the end of Israel and its implications for the Southern Kingdom of Judah. The second era was known as the *Neo-Babylonian* period, whose focus marked out the attendant circumstances and succeeding conditions of the fall of the Southern Kingdom in 586 B.C. The notable prophets of that time were Zephaniah, Jeremiah, Habakkuk, Nahum, Ezekiel, and Obadiah. The third period was known as the *post-exilic*. These prophets appeared during the Persian rule of the Jews and Cyrus' desire to free the Jews in 536 B.C., making things better for them. The prophets who make up this period are Daniel, Haggai, Zechariah, Joel, and Malachi.

This presents a brief but relevant look at the work of a genuine prophet of God. The Scriptures contain all we need to know about their work and influence over the people of Israel and to a greater extent, the world around them and where we stand today. The words of the prophets are to be a lesson in behavior and morals and most importantly, how to approach and worship a holy God who holds our lives in His hands. Before we venture further in our study, let us apply what has been written to the present day, especially in the churches. Scripture declares: "For the time has come for judgment to begin at the house of God, and if it begins with us first, what will be the end of those who do not obey the gospel of God?" (1 Peter 4:17, NKJV).

A pastor is the called under-shepherd of the church, responsible for feeding his people the good food of the Word. Those under his care are his flock. Often a pastor will preach on subjects like the tithe, discipleship, holiness, a disciplined life, and conforming to the person and work of Christ. All of this is designed to produce good fruit in the life of a believer. That pastor, if he is in tune to the direction of the Holy Spirit, will sometimes call for the need to have a repentant life and submit oneself to the Lordship of Christ. This style of prophetic preaching is the type that tends to "step on toes", especially if there is someone in the church who is not living a righteous life, knows it, but still plays the game of piety.

Church members tend to like when the pastor starts preaching about sins and the need to repent, except when the sins that they are secretly committing gets personal. The convicted members, now under the conviction of the Holy Spirit, may oppose the pastor's work and start criticizing him for petty reasons. The prophetic message that someone was hoping would correct the other member now applies to them and they do not like it. Many Bible-believing pastors have undergone seasons of resentment as a result. He should never minimize the message of the gospel. The souls of people are far too precious to let them think that all is well but are instead heading down the broad road that leads to destruction.

One troubling trend founding churches today are the people who think they're saved because they "made a decision for Christ" or "asked Jesus into their heart" (a term or teaching that is NEVER found in Scripture) or prayed a "sinner's prayer" (despite the fact that we're all sinners). There are people right now who are deluded into a false sense of security when all they have done is repeated words or phrases that they either did not bother to take seriously or clearly understand. Tragically, far too many people walking around in churches and in the world today honestly believe they are saved, but their lives produce no fruit or show signs of a holy, consecrated life devoted to Jesus Christ.

The modern church needs to stop and carefully examine any type of activity or teaching that minimizes the holiness, character, and glory of God. The time is long overdue to condemn little "sermonettes" that people might enjoy because they are not too lengthy and get out early in time to pursue another interest. The church needs to repent of its worldliness and desire to be "approved" by people and movements who are content with their unrepentant behaviors and refuse to change. We are not the world's friend, but instead are to be God- centered people who will reach out to the desperate, the spiritually hungry, the humble, the broken-hearted, the ones yearning for personal peace, and implore them to look to Jesus, be rescued from an eternity in hell and the consequences of a wasted and reprobate life. We are to preach like dying men as to reach dying men.

 We desperately need Jesus back in the church along with fearless preachers behind the pulpit who will present biblical grace to the humble and admonishment to the proud. We are running out of time. The house is on fire, and no one is turning on the hydrant, deciding instead to admire the design and machinery of the fire engine while the people scream for rescue. There is no excuse for anyone to sit by and watch the world fall into hell. Prophetic preaching done in the power of the Holy Spirit results in the production of fruitful and holy lives. It clears out the dross and helps to harvest the wheat.

The role of the biblically affirmed pastor cannot be minimized. He has been given the God-given authority to preach the Word of God with no compromise. In examining the duties of the prophet, there is an unmistakable sign and authority of the pastoral office in the pages of the New Testament (especially with our Lord Jesus) and those who have been specifically called to this sacred office throughout the history of the church. The charge to be a pastor/teacher is a sacred trust and office which should never be taken lightly or frivolously. He is answerable to the LORD for his words and actions and must show courage in the face of opposition both from his people and the world.

The pastor/teacher needs to emphasize that Jesus Christ is LORD. He is our Friend, but we are to also come to Him in an attitude of reverence and honor. There is little or no sense of holy respect for God by some pastors who tend to think of the Lord Jesus as a celestial buddy playing games with them in alleged dreams and visions. This is God in the flesh we are encountering! We should face Him as the apostle John did on Patmos (Revelation 1:17) and like Isaiah did when He saw the LORD in the temple (Isaiah 6:1-8). There is little if any real, authentic, reverent fear or respect of the Lord God Almighty in the church today, and that man who is called to a church as pastor and shepherd should be an example to his people in how to worship God in spirit and truth.

It is unmistakably obvious that we need genuine revival in this nation that will bring us to our knees and bow humbly in the presence of God and totally transform both the church and the nation into true and faithful servants. We need to return to the majesty and holiness of God with a reverent respect, awe, and a desire to totally submit and obey His sovereign will. We need to get it into our soul, heart, and mind that we can do absolutely nothing without Him. The Holy Spirit needs to remind us that we are helpless without His indwelling power.

It is the work of the Holy Spirit to convict us of our sins and to bring us into the presence of the living God (John 16:5-15). We should humble ourselves before the throne of the Lord Jesus Christ and ask Him to forgive us of our worldliness and compromise. We need an anointing of our souls to pursue the sure truth of the Word of God. We need to be spiritually hungry for the Living Bread and thirsty for the Water of Life. Time is running out. Now is the time and place to approach the LORD in prayer, seek the counsel of the Scriptures, and inquire what you need to do for His grace, honor, and glory and not necessarily what you want, desire, or request.

You need to come to the realization that the Sovereign God of all creation is not your butler who is always at your beck and call, eagerly waiting to prosper, bless ,favor, and serve you while the world travels down the wide road to eternal destruction. There have been too many godly servants who have suffered untold persecution and hardship over the centuries and have risked everything in this present time in to obtain the Word of God in countries where it is a crime, punishable by certain imprisonment or death to own a copy of the Scriptures. It will come here. Are you prepared for that probability?

Chapter 2
The Importance of Accurate Interpretation of the Biblical Text

It is one thing to say that someone is a student of biblical prophecy, but if they are not aware of how a passage of prophecy or Scripture for that matter is to be properly interpreted, then they may be in jeopardy of reading something into the passage that does not reflect sound investigation and study, but may be a product of their own bias or, at worst, fitting a section of Scripture into a belief that may not be orthodox in perspective. Our quest for spiritual maturity must be based upon the foundation of the apostles and prophets, with Jesus Christ being the chief cornerstone. He expects us to read and study the Word, allowing the Holy Spirit to draw our attention to passages that we may not like or find uninteresting, but may be used by him to teach us valuable lessons that are of benefit and growth.

We need to be students of the entirety of the Word and to do so means learning to properly interpret it. There is a science in the interpretation of the Bible, and it is part of learning the deep truths of God. God did not leave us floundering on our own in the realm of biblical study. We have the Holy Spirit as our teacher if we will but pray and ask Him to do so. Here are some verses to study that present the Holy Spirit as a teacher:

"But the Helper, the Holy Spirit whom the Father will send in My name, He will teach you all things, and bring to your remembrance all that I said to you" – John 14:26 (NASB)

"Which things we also speak, not in words taught in human wisdom, but in those taught by the Spirit, combining spiritual thoughts with spiritual words." – 1 Corinthians 2:13 (NASB)

"And when they arrest you and deliver you up, do not be anxious beforehand about what you are to say, but say whatever is given you in that hour; for it is not you who speaks, but it is the Holy Spirit" – Mark 13:11 (NASB)

"And as for you the anointing which you have received from Him abides in you and you have no need for anyone to teach you; but as His anointing teaches you about all things,

and is true, and is not a lie and just as it has taught you, you abide in Him" — *1 John 2:27 (NASB)*

The disciples and early followers of Jesus relied upon the Holy Spirit to help them recall everything the LORD had taught them over His brief period of ministry. There is no way that they could remember everything without the aid of the Holy Spirit, especially as time went on and the apostles were getting older. The Holy Spirit guided them and the next generation of believers to make accurate copies of the Gospels, the histories, the epistles, and the Apocalypse to instruct the growing church.

The teachings of the apostles were an accurate testimony and means of defense to fight the varied heresies that appeared not long after the church was established. The New Testament canon was finished around 90 – 95 A.D. with the last books being the apostle John's composition of his gospel, his three letters, and the book of Revelation. The original manuscripts of the New Testament writers were carefully copied over the next three hundred years. The copiers were usually laypeople who wanted a copy of the Scriptures for themselves or for a house church meeting in a city or countryside. It is a probable theory that the original manuscripts were kept safely and solemnly by pastors and teachers and probably survived for at least two hundred years after their writing.

This statement can be a sound hypothesis, for we possess biblical manuscripts dating from the second century AD. The body of believers that were scattered throughout the Roman Empire would be familiar with what was genuine and what was a teaching or opinion by a pastor, or at worst, a heretic. Heresies, as stated earlier, were rebutted and challenged by churches who had copies of the manuscripts, specifically in cities such as Antioch, Syria, Alexandria, Egypt, Constantinople in Asia Minor (modern day Turkey) Rome, and Greece.

To believe or state that the early Christians did not know the genuine Word from the fraudulent teachings of those who would twist the Scriptures for their own purposes is to assume ignorance on their part. Some Bible scholars who consider themselves skeptics often demean previous generations because they weren't as advanced as we are today or that they clung to alleged "superstitions" such as their affirmation of the resurrection of Christ or the accuracy of the varied manuscripts. Blood has been shed to preserve what God has said to us. Countless martyrs throughout the centuries courageously proclaimed that all people should have a copy of the Scriptures and paid for that conviction with their lives.

The surety of the Scriptures in the face of persecution is documented by New Testament scholar F.F. Bruce. In his work The Canon of Scripture (1), he says this about the church in this harrowing situation:

"At the beginning of the fourth century, there was one last outbreak of imperial persecution. On February 23, 303 A.D., an edict was ordered empire-wide for all the Christian Scriptures to be surrendered to the authorities for destruction. This was a new form of persecution, having to surrender Scripture. However, churches had copies of the Scriptures along with other sacred writings. The officials who demanded surrender really did not know which works were Scripture and what was not. The issue to consider is that by this time in church history, the people knew what authentic Scripture was compared to another Christian work. It is safe to say that by the time of the Emperor Constantine's Edict of Toleration in 313, legalizing Christianity, the New Testament canon was established and agreed upon by the Church Fathers."

There are critics of the Scriptures who say that because there are so many derivatives of words and phrase in manuscripts that we cannot be certain that what we have are the original words written by the apostles. It is a fair question to consider and is worthy of examination. Has the Bible we have today been altered or corrupted? Critics will tell us that the original manuscripts are long gone, probably confiscated and burned with other manuscripts during the outbreaks of imperial persecution or simply became too fragile to survive the ravages of time. It is true that all we have are copies of copies. We need to address this issue and rightfully conclude that the Scripture we have now has been faithfully copied and affirmed over the centuries.

The first set of manuscripts and copies to examine is the Old Testament itself. The truth is that the original writings are long gone and were off the scene during the four hundred "silent years" when God did not reveal any new teaching or admonition to His people. How did the words that we know today as the Old Testament stay preserved? Three sources give credibility to the authenticity of the text. The first source relevant to preservation is referred to as the Masoretic Text, which is a collection of Old Testament works that date back to 900 A.D. The scholars who worked on this text were called Masorites, who took the existing Hebrew text and added vowel markings for easier reading and understanding, which became the Hebrew language and composition used for research and study today.

Comparisons with earlier Greek and Latin translations reveal careful copying with little deviation between 100 B.C. and 900 A.D.

There needs to be a word about the Jewish scribe, the appointed official who copied the words that we refer to as the Old Testament. To copy God's sacred revelation was not something the scribe took lightly. There was a reverence for the holy and it is said that when the scribe came to the word representing the name of God, he washed himself before writing down the holy name. Any error was cause for the entire scroll to be discarded and buried, for burning it would have been an insult to God. They realized that what they were doing was not merely an exercise in writing, but something solemn and reverent. The other texts for examination are the writings known as the <u>Dead Sea Scrolls</u> which were composed between150 B.C. -70 A.D. These scrolls were composed by a sect of Jews known as Essenes, who wrote teachings on the coming war between the "Sons of Light" and the "Sons of Darkness".

The Essenes were apocalyptic in their outlook on the world but were also meticulous copiers of the Scriptures. They lived in a desert community known as Qumran, near the Dead Sea, and were contemporaries of John the Baptist, who may have lived with them while he was growing up after the death of his parents, Zacharias and Elizabeth (Luke 1). The Essenes did not interact with the society of that day because they believed that it was too corrupt. They wrote copies of every Old Testament book except Esther and continued to exist as a group until the Roman invasion of Judea in 70 A.D. The Jews had been rebelling against Roman rule for four years and the Roman commander, Titus, was determined to crush the rebellion once and for all, destroying Jerusalem and the Temple, just as Jesus had predicted (Matthew 24: 15-28; Mark 13:14-23; Luke 21:20-24). Jews were massacred and the Essenes were no exception. They hid their writings in jars and placed them in the caves surrounding Qumran. They were victims of Rome's fury as well and the scrolls were forgotten for nearly 2,000 years.

Then In 1947, a Bedouin Arab shepherd letting his flocks graze near the area of Qumran threw a rock into one of the caves and heard something break. He went into the cave and discovered several large clay jars that were sealed. The jar that was broken held scrolls. He took a handful of them and went to Jerusalem to an antiquities dealer to see if he could get money for his find. The dealer asked him where he had gotten the scrolls and was given directions to the caves. The dealer and textual scholars got a hold of the jars and carefully unwrapped the scrolls, some fracturing into small bits.

The scholars began to unwrap a fifty -foot scroll, which turned out to be the complete text of the prophet Isaiah. It turned out that the copy and the Masoretic text were alike. The careful copying of the Old Testament through the centuries had been proven accurate. The scrolls are in The Israel Museum in Jerusalem.

The third source we have for Old Testament accuracy is the Greek translation of the Scriptures made in 200 B.C. by seventy scholars who translated the Hebrew into Greek, which was the official language of the known world of that time, initiated by the conquests of Alexander the Great, who made the world affluent in Greek culture, art, philosophy, religion, and language. This translation is known as the Septuagint and is an accurate record just as is the Masoretic text of the medieval world, with little criticism from present-day biblical scholars on the accuracy of the Hebrew text.

What can be said about the New Testament that we have today? Objective sources and critical examinations of the existing manuscripts point to a continual preservation of the original writings. Sufficient evidence exists to verify this claim and its defense in the face of skepticism from both religious and secular critics. In his book More Evidence That Demands a Verdict (2), apologist Josh McDowell presents the following data on New Testament manuscript reliability:

"There are now more than 5, 686 known Greek Manuscripts of the New Testament. Add over 10,000 Latin Vulgate (The Scriptures in Latin) and at least 9,300 other early versions (M55) and we have close to, if not more than 25,000 manuscripts of the New Testament in existence today. No other document of antiquity even begins to approach such numbers and attestations. Here is a breakdown of the number of surviving manuscripts (MSS) of the New Testament:

- *Extant Greek Manuscripts*

   Uncials (Manuscripts in capital letters without spaces, which was the way most documents were written then) -307

   Minuscule (small letters/fragments) -2,860

   Lectionaries (Church compilations of Scripture for teaching and reading) – 2,410

   Papyri (copies of preserved works) – 109

   Total – 5,686

- Manuscripts in Other Languages:

- Latin Vulgate -10,000

- Ethiopic – 2,000

- Slavic -4,101

- Arminian -2,587

- Syria - Pashtu -350

- Buhari – 100

- Arabic -75

- Old Latin -50

- Anglo Saxon – 7

- Gothic – 6

- Sogdian – 3

- Old Syrian -2

- Persian -2

- Frankish – 1

Total: 19,284

Grand Total: 24,970

Bruce Metzger (1914 -2005), considered one of the greatest experts on the New Testament manuscripts, presents the following testimony to New Testament accuracy in his volume <u>The Oxford Companion to the Bible (3):</u>
"The oldest known New Testament manuscript is a papyrus fragment measuring 3 ½ x 2 ½ inches dated from 100 -150 A.D. which preserves five verses from John 18, P52, as it is labeled, is now kept at the John Ryland's Library in Manchester, England. "

"The oldest substantial portions of the New Testament are the Bodmer papyrus of John (P86), now in Geneva, Switzerland, and the Chester Beatty papyri (P46) in Dublin and Ann Arbor, which contain ten Pauline letters, dated to 200 A.D. The oldest parchment New Testament copies are Codex Vatican and Codex Sinaiticus (4th

Century). From roughly 300 -1000 A.D., about 300 manuscripts remain, and from 1000 -1500 A.D., about 2000 copies have survived."

On his website Cold Case Christianity (4) former homicide detective and current Christian apologist J. Warner Wallace presents the following affirmation about historical reliability: *"I researched the writings of the generations of Christian students who followed the original New Testament authors. These early church fathers sat at the feet of the apostles and learned from the eyewitness accounts. These secondary leaders then wrote letters and documents of their own, repeating the claims of their teachers. From the non-canonical works of Ignatius and Polycarp (students of John) and Clement (a student of Paul) we can determine the following:*

- *Jesus was predicted by the Old Testament as described in the New Testament.*

- *Jesus is divine as taught in the New Testament.*

- *Jesus taught His disciples as described in the New Testament.*

- *Jesus worked miracles as described in the New Testament.*

- *Jesus was born of a virgin as described in the New Testament.*

- *Jesus lived, ministered, was crucified and died as described in the New Testament.*

- *Jesus rose from the dead and demonstrated His duty as described in the New Testament.*

The early disciples of the apostles confirm the content of the apostolic teaching. The early church fathers confirm this for us, even if they don't repeat every bit of the canonical narrative."

Mark D. Roberts, writing on his blog on www.patheos.com (5) has a series on can we know what the original gospel manuscripts really said? His observations square with conservative, orthodox scholarship. He goes on to say the following: *"Let us think for a moment about what might allow us to put confidence in the manuscripts of the Gospels:*

First, we would look for antiquity. We would want the manuscripts in existence to be old, the closer to the autographs, the better. The less time between the originals and the existing copies decreases the possibility of changes being introduced through many acts of copying.

Second, we would prefer multiplicity. Clearly it would be better to have many manuscripts at our disposal rather than just a few. More manuscripts would put us in a much better position to determine the original wording.

Third, we would want trustworthy scholarly methodology. If the academics who study the biblical manuscripts, known as textual critics, utilize reliable methods, one that maximizes objectivity, then we would have greater confidence in their conclusions.

Fourth, we would look at the quantity and quality of textually ambiguous passages made up of differences called variants among the manuscripts. If the existing copies of the gospels contain a high proportion of textual variants, then we would have less confidence in our ability to access the content of the autographs. If it turns out that the existing manuscripts are filled with all sorts of significant textual disagreements, then we would question our knowledge of what was originally written. If, on the contrary, the differences among existing manuscripts are relatively insignificant, then we'd rightly place confidence in the central Greek text upon which translations are based."

This is just the surface of objective Biblical and historical verification. There is noteworthy evidence to confirm that what has been written and recorded through the centuries is the inerrant word of God. But what about sources outside of the Bible record? Does secular history record the life of Jesus? After all, He was a Jewish peasant living in a remote corner of the Roman Empire in an area governed by a Roman appointed tetrarch and district official appointed by Tiberius Caesar. Critics used to speculate that there was little evidence of Jesus' life outside the Gospels. In response to this claim, Dr. Norman Geisler, former Dean of the Southern Evangelical Seminary wrote <u>The Popular Handbook of Archaeology and the Bible</u> (6) and presented Roman historical records showing that this is not true. He wrote:

"Arguments denying the existence of Jesus of Nazareth have fallen out of favor due to the growing body of documentary evidence from Jewish and Greco-Roman sources that speak of Jesus and the events surrounding His life and ministry. From these early non-Christian sources such as Flavius Josephus, the Babylonian Talmud, Pliny the Younger, Tacitus, Mari Ben Serpin, Suetonius, Thallus, Lucian, and Celsius, we may reconstruct the salient features of the life of Christ without appealing to the New Testament. These features include the following:

- *Jesus lived during the reign of Tiberius Caesar.*

- *He lived a virtuous life.*

- *He was a wonder worker.*

- *He had a brother named James.*

- *He was claimed to be the Messiah.*

- *He was crucified under Pontius Pilate.*

- *He was crucified on the eve of the* Passover.

- *Darkness and an earthquake occurred when He died*

- *His disciples believed He had risen from the dead.*

- *His disciples were willing to die for their beliefs.*

- *Christianity spread as far as Rome.*

- *Christian disciples denied the Roman gods and worshipped Jesus as God.*

From these facts, we can have confidence in that what we have are the genuine words and commandments of God and the reality of Jesus Christ. Now we come to another part of our journey. How are the Scriptures to be interpreted of what was just presented? The first thing that needs to be done is define the word "interpretation". The 1828 Webster's Dictionary (7) says that interpretation is *"the act of interpreting, explanation of unintelligible words in language, the design of translation; the act of expounding or unfolding what is not understood, such as dreams or prophecy. It can also mean exposition, such as varied interpretations of portions of Scripture; the power of explaining."*

Specific terms need to be defined before going further. First, the term literal means "that which accords with the letter" (8). In his thoroughly researched volume on end time prophecy entitled Things to Come (9), Dr. J. Dwight Pentecost, late Professor of Biblical Studies at Dallas Theological Seminary, gave his convictions about the necessity of proper literal interpretation:

"The literal method of interpretation is that method that gives to each word the same exact basic meaning it would have in normal, ordinary, customary usage, whether employed in writing, speaking, or thinking. It is referred to as the grammatical-historical method to emphasize the fact that the meaning is to be determined by both historical and grammatical considerations."

He goes on to give another definition of literal interpretation and its evidence: *"The literal method is the customary, socially acknowledged designation of a word. The literal meaning of a word is the basic, customary, social designation of that*

31

word. The spiritual or mystical meaning of a word or expression is one that arises after the literal designation and is dependent upon it for its existence." The evidence for the literal method has six notable characteristics:

"1) The literal meaning of sentences is the normal approach in all languages.

2) All secondary meanings of documents, parables, types, allegories (defined as any statement of supposed facts which admits of a literal interpretation and yet requires or justly admits of a moral or figurative statement), and symbols, depend on this very existence on the previous literal meaning of the term.

3) The greater part of the Bible makes adequate sense when interpreted literally.

4) The literalist approach does not rule out figures of speech, symbols, allegories, and types, but if the nature of the sentence so demands, it readily yields to the second sense.

- *This method is the only sane and safe check on the imaginations of people.*

- *This method is the only one consistent with the nature of inspiration. The plenary inspiration of the Bible teaches that the Holy Spirit guided men into truth and away from error. In this process the Spirit of God used language, and the units of language (as meaning, not as sound) as words and thoughts. The thought is the thread that strings the words together. Therefore, our very exegesis must commence with a study of words and grammar, the two foundations of all meaningful speech."*

What are some examples of literal interpretation? Read Daniel 8:2-8 (KJV):

"2) And I saw in a vision; and it came to pass, when I saw, that I was at Shushan in the palace, which is in the province of Elam; and I saw in a vision, and I was by the river of Ulla.(3) Then I lifted up mine yes, and saw, and behold, there stood before the river a ram which had two horns: and the two horns were high; but one was higher than the other, and the higher came up last. (4) I saw the ram pushing westward, and northward, and southward; do that no beasts might stand before him, neither was there any that could deliver out of his hand; but he did according to his will and became great. (5) As I was considering, behold, a goat came from the west on the face of the whole earth, and touched not the ground; and the goat had a notable horn between his eyes. (6) And he came to the ram that had two horns, which I had seen standing before the river, and ran into him in the fury of his power. (7) And I saw him come close unto the ram, and he was moved with choler (anger) against him, and smote the ram, and brake his two horns, and there was no power in the ram to stand before him, but he cast him down to

the ground, and stamped upon him, and there was none that could deliver the ram out of his hand. (8) Therefore, the male goat waxed very great; and when he was strong, the great horn was broken; and for it came up four notable ones toward the four winds of heaven."

Understanding this passage begins with examining ancient history and those specific kingdoms that were about to come on the world stage. This where the use of valuable study tools comes in, such as biblical commentaries, written by varied experts who take books of the Bible by chapter and verse and present a sensible interpretation of what the author of the Scriptural text has written, using historical events to assist in the meaning of the Biblical account. It is important to examine and verify one's sources of information. It is an advantage to obtain more conservative and objective material in order to clearly understand and analyze what has been written in the Word of God. Some passages are self-explanatory while others need to have some background information.

It is worth examining other interpretations concerning this style of prophetic writing. One interpretation comes from the late John Walvoord (1910-2002), who was the President of Dallas Theological Seminary, along with being one of the most notable prophecy scholars of the last century, writing numerous books and papers on this topic. He wrote a popular commentary on the Old Testament book of Daniel. (10), and gives a historical interpretation of Daniel's vision in Chapter 8:

"vv. 1 -2: The vision occurred in the third year of Belshazzar's reign (he was co-regent with his father Nabonidus in Babylon). This was twelve years before the feast of Chapter 5 that brought down the Babylonian Empire in 532 B.C. In the vision that Daniel had while awake, he was transported to the city of Susa, 150 miles north of the Persian Gulf and 225 Miles east of Babylon. Susa would play an important role because it would become the capital of what would be the Persian Empire.

vv. 3 -4; A two horned ram, with one horn more dominant than the other, appears on the scene. This symbolizes the rapid growth and expansion of the Persian Empire. The one horn represents the Medes, and the stronger horn represented the Persians. The empire spread rapidly northward, southward, and westward, overrunning Babylon and extending to the Mediterranean, including Egypt, Asia Minor (Turkey), and what was the land of Israel prior to the exile in 586 B.C. The Persians would be the dominant power for over two hundred years (532 -331 B.C.)

vv. 5 -7: The male goat with one horn appears on the scene, representing the king of Greece coming from the west. This refers to the rise and conquests of Alexander the Great

(356 -322 B.C.). He overran the ram in a blitzkrieg of power, destroying it. He conquered the Persians at the Battle of Issus in 331 B.C. Alexander's empire would include all the territory of Persia, Greece, Egypt, Israel, and at the border of India. He was the ruler of the known world, having conquered the territory in just a few years. Alexander would spread Greek art, culture, philosophy (he had been tutored by the great philosopher Aristotle), and language. It was Greek that was one of the official languages of what would become the Roman Empire, and the language in which the New Testament was written.

v. 8: Alexander's reign would not last long. As symbolized by the breaking of the horn. He died of a fever at the age of 33 in 322 B.C. Not long after his death, a power struggle as to who would rule the empire comes into play. Final control would be at the hands of his trusted generals, who divided the empire into four kingdoms. The kingdoms that would play a role in Jewish history would be the kingdom of Egypt and the west, ruled by Ptolemy and his descendants until its conquest by Rome in 31 B.C. The other kingdom was ruled by Seleucid and his descendants until the Jewish revolt under the Maccabees in 163 B.C.

Other sources such as the <u>Believer's Bible Commentary</u> (11) refer to the same historical interpretation. Author William MacDonald states: *"Daniel had a vision of a ram and a male goat. The ram was Persia, and the two horns represented the combined kingdoms of Media and Persia. One horn was higher than the other, representing the power of the Persian rulers. The ram was on a rampage, moving northward, westward, and south, and the ram was irresistible, such was its power and swiftness. The male, one horned goat represented Greece. He came from the west rapidly and powerfully. The one horn represents the conqueror Alexander the Great, who overran the Persians and captured their empire, along with Greece and the west, including all of Asia Minor and the Indus River, west of India. When Alexander died, his empire was divided into four parts, each ruled by one of his generals, represented by the four notable horns."*

Gleason Archer, writing in <u>The Expositor's Bible Commentary</u> (12) presents his analysis: *"Media/Persia is represented as a ram with two horns, one larger than the other, representing the domination of the Persians over the Medes. This also represents the bear of Chapter 7, verse 5. The larger horn came later, even as Cyrus and his Persians come later than the rulers of Medea. The empire spread north, west, and south rapidly. A swift, one horned goat emerges with one mighty charge that destroys the ram. In 334, the forces of Alexander the Great overran Persia. Within three years, Alexander's empire reached into what is now Afghanistan and east of the border of India. His rule as sole emperor came to a sudden halt when he died of a fever in 323 B.C. His four generals seized control and divided the empire into four parts, with Ptolemy ruling Egypt and the west, and Seleucid ruling the region of Syria and the East, which was significant in Jewish history."*

The Scriptures clearly identify the nations which represent the ram and the goat:

"(19) And he said, Behold, I will make thee know what shall be in the last end of the indignation; for at the time appointed the end shall be. (20) The ram which thou saw having two horns are the kings of Media and Persia. (21) And the rough goat is the king of Greece; and the great horn that is between his eyes is the first king. (22) Now that being broken, whereas four stood up for it, four kingdoms shall stand up out of the nation, but not in his power." (KJV)

Literal interpretation is Scripture interpreting Scripture, and is referred to as <u>exegesis</u>, the study of Scripture using methods of inquiry such as the original biblical languages of Hebrew and Greek, commentaries, dictionaries, books on biblical theology and doctrine, concordances, and a good study Bible Exegesis is not just for the pastor or scholar, but for all those who want to discover the riches of Scripture.

Now we come to a problem in the interpretation of Scripture referred to as <u>eisegesis</u>. Where exegesis is discovering what the Scripture says through methods of study, eisegesis is making the text say what you want it to say and not what it is meant to say originally. These are verses, for example, which define a doctrine or a teaching with which there is disagreement. The world uses eisegesis for specific Scriptures as a defense or excuse to justify a respective lifestyle or worldview. One verse that has been taken out of context as a result of bad interpretation is found in the Sermon on the Mount. It is Matthew 7:1, which is smugly quoted when confronted or questioned. It is *"Judge not, that ye be not judged" (KJV)*. That is as far as they care to read. It might be the only verse they know and use in a manner that is way out of context.

Let us look at Verses 1 -6, which gives the whole teaching, and in examining it, rebukes the ignorance and arrogance of these people: *"Judge not, that ye be not judged. For with what judgment ye judge, ye shall be judged, and with what measure hand it out, it shall be measured to you again. And why behold thou the speck that is in thy brother's eye, but consider not the beam that is thine own eye? Or how wilt thou say to thy brother, let me pull out the mote (speck) out of thine eye; and behold, a beam is in thine own eye? Hypocrite! First cast out the beam out of thine own eye; and then shalt thou see clearly to cast out the mote out of the brother's eye. Give not that which is holy to the dogs, neither cast ye your pearls before swine, lest they trample them under their feet and turn against you and tear you." (KJV)*

Writing on these passages, William MacDonald, once again from the Believer's Bible Commentary (13) says the following. It is lengthy but well worth noting: *"Sometimes these words of our LORD are misconstrued by people to prohibit all forms of judgment. No matter what happens, they piously say "Judge not, that you be not judged". But Jesus is not teaching that we are to be undiscerning Christians. He never intended that we abandon our critical faculty or discernment. The New Testament has many illustrations of legitimate judgment of the condition, conduct, or teaching of others. In addition, there are several areas in which the Christian is commanded to decide, and to discriminate between good and bad or between good and best. Some of these include:*

- *When disputes arise between believers, they should be settled in the church before members who can decide the matter (1 Corinthians 6:1-8).*

- *The local church is to judge serious sins of its members and take appropriate action (Matthew 18:17; 1 Corinthians 5:9-13).*

- *Believers are to judge the doctrinal teaching of teachers and preachers by the Word of God (Matthew &:15-20; 1 Corinthians 14:29; 1 John 4:1).*

- *Christians must discern if others are believers in order to obey Paul's command in 2 Corinthians 6: 14.*

- *Those in the church must judge which men have the qualifications necessary for elders and deacons (1 Timothy 3: 1-13).*

- *We must discern which people are unruly, fainthearted, weak, etc. and treat them according to the instructions in the Bible (1 Thessalonians 5:14).*

Jesus warned that unrighteous judgment would be repaid in kind (v.2). This principle of reaping what we sow is built into all human life and affairs. Jesus exposed our tendency to see a small fault in someone else while ignoring the same fault in ourselves. He purposely exaggerated the situation to drive home the point. Someone with a plank in their eye often finds fault with someone who has a speck in their eye, not even noticing his own condition. It is hypocritical to suppose that we could help someone with a fault when we ourselves have a greater fault. We must remedy our own faults before criticizing them in others. Verse 6 proves that Jesus did not intend to forbid every kind of judgment. He wanted His disciples to not give holy things to dogs or throw pearls before swine. Under the Mosaic Law dogs and swine were unclean animals and here the term is used to depict wicked people. When we meet certain individuals, who treat divine truths with utter contempt and respond to our preaching of the claims of Christ with abuse and violence, we are not obligated to continue to share the gospel with them. To press the matter only brings increased condemnation to the offenders."

In his commentary on Matthew (14), John Walvoord says this about vv.1-6:

"The opening words of Chapter 7 have become a mantra in today's permissive culture. Many people who do not know any other part of the Bible have committed the first half of verse 1 to memory! These words are used to prevent any criticism of a person's behavior as if this pronouncement from Jesus bans all forms of discernment and evaluation. This is not the meaning of this exhortation. The reason this text cannot be made to say we are never to judge are quite simple and obvious. First, in verse 6, which immediately follows Jesus' teaching on judgment (non-hypocritical) in verses 1-4, Jesus continue by saying, 'Do not give dogs what is sacred; do not throw your pearls to pigs."

We must examine ourselves before we can cast a critical eye on others. Also, we are not to waste our time with those who blatantly mock or curse the gospel. They will be judged by the Lord Jesus Himself on the great and terrible day of the LORD (Matthew 25:41-46; Revelation 20:11-15). Other commentators tell us that Jesus forbids judgment on people when you do not know their circumstances, using your own ideas of how they are to believe and behave. We are to look to Scripture as our guideline. Anything else is of the flesh and is not becoming a true child of God.

Chapter 3
The Importance of Christian Doctrine

What we believe as Christians is as important as why we are Christians in the first place. At one time we were rebels against God, then someone told us about Jesus, or we watched a program on television, heard a broadcast on the radio, or we were just curious and came across a website or article that gave a defense of Christianity and the importance of belief in Jesus Christ as Lord and Savior. The Holy Spirit convicted us of our sins, and we turned to Jesus and asked Him to save us, devoting our lives to Him in the process. That is how the beginning of the Christ-centered life should proceed. There are basic beliefs every Christian should possess. These beliefs are called fundamentals.

The website www.disepensationalberean.com presents these beliefs that should be affirmed by everyone who considers themselves a child of God and upon which we should agree. They are:

The deity of our Lord Jesus Christ (John 1:1; 20:28; Hebrews 1: 8-9). Who is the Creator God Himself (Ephesians 3:9; Colossians 1:16; Genesis 1:1); Who laid the foundation of the earth (Hebrews 1: 10-12; Psalm 102:24-27); The Virgin Birth (Isaiah 7:14; Matthew 1:23; Luke 1:27); The Blood Atonement (Acts 20:28; Romans 3:25; 5:9; Ephesians 1:7; Hebrews 9:12-14) Note: This refers to a belief in salvation by grace alone (Sola Gratia) through faith alone (Sola Fide) in the Blood of Christ. Romans 3:25 states that set forth Jesus to be a propitiation through faith in His Blood. Romans 5:9 states that we are justified by the blood of Christ and Ephesians 1:7 states that we have redemption through His blood. Another fundamental of the faith is the fact of the bodily Resurrection of Jesus Christ from the dead (Luke 24:36-46; 1 Corinthians 15: 1-4, 14-15), and the inerrancy of the Scriptures themselves (Psalm 12: 6-7; Romans 15:4; 2 Timothy 3:16-17; 1 Peter 1:19-21). We are rely on Scripture alone (sola scriptura). There is no ground for any "new" revelation. The Scriptures are sufficient and complete. (1)

The child of God who wishes to mature in their walk with the LORD needs to know and study the essential teachings of the Christian faith, and to set a mindset that reflects the challenge that Paul gave to Timothy in order that the young pastor would be able to teach the truth about the Lord Jesus (2 Timothy 2:15; Acts 17:11).

Another term for doctrinal study is theology, defined as "Divinity, the science of God and divine things, or the science which teaches the existence, character, and attributes of God, His laws and the duties we are to practice. Theology consists of two branches, natural and revealed. Natural theology is the knowledge we have of God from His works by the light of nature and reason, while revealed theology is that which is to be learned only from revelation." (2)

The branch of theology that presents a more detailed study of the Christian life is known as systematic theology. "Systematic" refers to something being put into a system. Systematic theology is, therefore, the division of theology into systems that explain its various areas. For example, many books of the Bible give us information about angels. Systematic theology takes all the information about angels from all the books of the Bible and organizes it into a system called angelology. That is what systematic theology is all about – organizing the teachings of the Bible. The following studies are representations of systematic thought (3):

• The study of God the Father and His characteristic is called Theology proper.

• The study of God the Son, the Lord Jesus Christ is called Christology.

• Pneumatology is the study of the Person and work of the Holy Spirit.

• The study of the Holy Scriptures is known as Bibliology.

• The doctrine of the act and benefits of salvation is known as Soteriology.

• The study of the office and function of the church is called Ecclesiology.

• Eschatology is the study of last things and the end of days.

- Demonology is the study of the persons and sinister work of fallen angels from a Christian perspective.

- The study of sin and its effects upon humanity and the world is known as Hamartiology.

- Angelology, as mentioned above, is the study of God's messengers from heaven.

- Anthropology is the study of man in his original as well as fallen state.

Systematic theology is an important tool in helping us to understand and teach the Bible in an organized manner. Each of these categories is worthy of examination and they all interact with one another. An example of systematic theology that might be of help in knowing doctrine is listed below. It would be to your benefit to study and pray over these and ask the LORD to give you the wisdom to live by these truths.

God is all powerful, the Creator of all things, the sustainer of life, the One who has all things under His control, who provides salvation for His people, who knows everything, is everywhere. You cannot escape from Him. He is altogether lovely, altogether worthy of our worship and praise. He can deliver us from trouble (Daniel 3:17), He can fulfill all righteous promises (Romans 4:21), to do exceedingly abundantly (Ephesians 3:20), to subdue all things (Philippians 3:21), to guard the soul's treasure (2 Timothy 1:12). He can pardon (Matthew 9:6) He keeps us from falling spiritually (Jude 24). He has plans for every one of us and will not share His glory with anyone else. He is the Lord God of heaven and Earth, and His will shall always be done for now and eternity.

Jesus Christ is Lord of heaven and Earth and all people throughout history will bow before Him (Philippians 2: 5-11). He is all powerful to save and deliver us from our sins. He lived a perfect, sinless life while here on Earth. He is the only begotten son of the Living God (John 3:16). He is virgin born (Isaiah 7:14). He is the promise of prophecy of the Old Testament and the fulfillment of it in the New (Luke 24:25-27). His death on the Cross was the accepted payment for our sins, and nothing else must be done. We are saved by faith in His finished work of salvation. He rose from the dead on third day just as He promised and now reigns from heaven in the lives and hearts of those who follow Him. He will return to Earth one day to rule and reign as King of Kings and Lord of Lords (Revelation 19:11-21).

The Holy Spirit is God. He is the Helper, who convicts people of their sins, and proclaims righteousness in the life of a believer (John 16: 8-15). He is the Author of Scripture (2 Peter 1: 21). He pours out His wisdom and power upon believers (Luke 24:49, Acts 1:5). He brought about the birth of the church by baptizing the 120 into His power, giving them supernatural signs and wonders (Acts 2) to show an unbelieving world the truth of the Gospel. He is our Teacher (1 John 2:27) and will never leave us. He points people to Christ and seeks to place within each believer gifts used to build up the church and to glorify God, never for personal edification. He will be a part of the new heaven and earth.

The Holy Bible is God's revelation of Himself to man and is written without any type of error or insufficient instruction. God the Holy Spirit inspired men to write the Bible and what we have is a perfect record of words and deeds done by God and men, both in their sinful and redeemed stages. The Bible is the final authority for instruction, reproof, doctrine, and correction (2 Timothy 3:16-17, John 17:17). It is the source of absolute permanent truth (Matthew 24:35). A person may come to faith in Christ by reading its words and be transformed by what is read. Again, nothing else needs to be added to the Scriptures. The canon is closed and there is no need of any or additional "new revelation".

The church is Jesus Christ's representation here on Earth. It is made up of those who have recognized their sins, asked for forgiveness, and have asked Jesus Christ to be their Lord and Savior. They are to place themselves under the leadership of a God-called, male, Bible-believing pastor as well as qualified elders (1 Timothy 3:1-8), who is commissioned to teach and preach the whole counsel of God (1Timothy 2:12). The members of a church are not to just take in instruction one day a week, but to interact with one another in fellowship and support. The church is made up of fallible people, who, too often, have made the church a place of cultural relevance instead of the body of Christ. Still, it is the body of Christ and will be made glorious and triumphant over the world, the flesh, and the devil (Romans 12:5; 1 Corinthians 10:17; 12:13; Ephesians 1:23; 4:12; 1 Peter 2:10).

Man was originally created in the image of God to serve and have communion with Him. While in Eden, man rebelled against the rule of God (Genesis 3) and became dead in sin and alienated from God. There is no way he can ever save himself, nor does he desire to do so in his fallen state (Romans 1:18-32; 3:10 -18). The only way that man can be reconciled with God is by an act of God Himself. The Bible clearly states that it is God who does the saving. (Romans 5:6-11). We have nothing to do with our salvation. Only by submitting himself to the Lordship of Jesus Christ does he have any hope of redemption and unity with Him. If we are truly His, we should always rejoice that He has seen fit to save and call us out of sin.

All people who die without Christ or who have denounced God throughout history will end up in a horrible place called hell. Satan and his demons are destined for that place at the end of history (Isaiah 14:12-17; Ezekiel 28:11-19; Matthew 25:41; Revelation 20:10) as well as the wicked of all time. If you end up there, it is a place without hope, mercy, grace, compassion, care, or love, for all eternity. Those who accept Christ as Lord and Savior will be ushered into His presence for all eternity where there is love, compassion, grace, mercy and love, and His presence forever (Luke 22:30; John 14:2; Philippians 3:20; 1 Peter 1:4; Revelation 21:27).This world is heading towards an end as we know it and will not get better.

The Scriptures warns us about these times (2 Timothy 3:1-8; 2 Peter 3:1-13, Matthew 24) and directs us to watch for the signs of His coming. The study of eschatology and prophetic inquiry go hand in hand. It has elements of each study. We see the Trinity being glorified, the church's triumph, the verification of Scripture, the surety of our salvation, our destiny established with the forces of evil defeated and above all, Jesus Christ being glorified in the entire drama of redemption. Ever since the 1970's with the publication of Hal Lindsey's classic The Late Great Planet Earth, the rise in interest about the end of all things has been on a lot of people's minds.

Movies have been made about Bible prophecy, people have taught it in seminars and Bible conferences, a plethora of books and tracts have centered on it, and it is a sure way to engage in colorful conversation with believer and non-believer alike. Opinions differ on interpretation, and those differences should not be a cause for division or question of one's salvation. Prophecy, like everything else in Scripture, needs to be examined and studied. Yet many churches do not do so and thee question is why? Here are a series of reasons why this topic is not touched by a lot of pastors.

Preachers want to "tickle ears" and preach about relevant, self-edifying topics and thus, shy away from controversy (2 Timothy 4:1-4; Hebrews 3: 10 -13). They see it as "too difficult to understand" and avoid it to not bring about discord. They want to "play it safe". Many were not taught prophecy in Bible College or seminary because it was deemed irrelevant, or a non-issue reserved for conspiracy theorists or other fringe thinkers. Never mind the fact that the Bible is 27% prophecy. Sadly, there are preachers who simply do not believe the Bible. They do not see it as the word of God, powerful and inerrant. They are, quite frankly, apostates (Jude 4, 12-17).

Authentic God- called preachers of the Gospel of Jesus Christ are to fearlessly and powerfully proclaim the "whole counsel" of God's word, even the teachings that upset people, and the question is why they get upset. Here are some blunt reasons why Bible preaching is not welcome or revered in the world and unfortunately, more and more churches in this day of growing apostasy and unbelief:

- Bible teaching and prophecy means that man is not in charge of the events that will bring history as we know it to an end.

- It shows that there will be an end to sinful pleasures. You will not be able to get away with it. Your time will come.

- It shows that we are accountable to God for our words and works.

- It shows that God's way will be accomplished despite what we do or say.

- It shows that Jesus Christ is the only way to heaven (John 14:6). All our ways are for nothing.

- It shows that God wins and there will be rewards for the obedient and punishment for the wicked.

- It shows that evil in all its forms will no longer be tolerated or welcomed. It will be eliminated along with all who practice it.

- It destroys any hope we have in ourselves to be able to overcome our own faults.

- It shows that people and nations will bow to Jesus Christ (Phil. 2:9-11).

- It makes way for a new heaven and a new earth (Revelation Chapters. 21 and 22)

As noted earlier, prophecy is an effective tool for evangelism and is designed to wake the sinner up. However, there is another branch of theology that is often overlooked by believers, and that bears examination. It is the theology of <u>apologetics</u>, which is defined as a rational, logical defense of the Christian faith. It is based upon Scriptures such as Philippians 1:16-17, 27; 1 Peter 3:15, and Jude 1:3.

We are to be able to present our testimony with boldness and to use the Scriptures as our line of defense, along with knowledge of relevant topics as directed by the LORD. Apologetics is not arguing someone into the kingdom of heaven, nor as a battering ram for ridiculing someone's unbelief using emotion as a weapon. It is not apologizing to the world for what you believe as a Christian. Apologetics requires study, faith, and reliance upon the Holy Spirit to convict the person in question about the seriousness of their sins and turn to the LORD for salvation. Apologetics can include studying such topics as manuscript evidence (which has been presented earlier, the study of philosophy, biology, mathematics, and logic.

For example, here are some questions that are often used by Christian apologists that you may find interesting and thought provoking:

1) If evolution is true and all we are essentially sophisticated animals, then where in the evolutionary journey did we start to believe that there may just be something or someone higher than we are?

2) If evolution is mere chance, then why does everything seem to be designed and work according to fixed natural laws? Why isn't there direct evidence of an evolving species? If science is progressing, then why are scientists holding on to an old theory that really has not shown much direct evidence?

3) Why is there microevolution but not evidence of macroevolution? Is there empirical evidence for evolution? Can it be observed in a laboratory using the scientific method?

4) If society determines morality, then how do you explain the Nazis and Communists whose morality was objectionable by any decent standards?

5) How do you explain the fact that the universe had a beginning? What or who brought it about? If truth is relative and it is whatever you want it to be, then how do you explain the accuracy of mathematics? Apologetics is not a weapon used to beat someone into submission to your point of view. It can be either defensive or offensive. Philippians 1: 7 says: "*Even as it is proper for me to think this of you all, because I have you in my heart in as much as both in my bonds, and in the defense and confirmation of the gospel, you are all partakers of my grace (KJV)*".

Chapter 4
Historical Developments that Shaped Christian Apologetics

The defense of the faith is emphasized in Scripture (Acts 4:12,20; 1 Peter 3:15) and was of vital importance to the early church, especially when they were facing an inhospitable government, rank paganism, hostility by society, and false information as to who Christians were and why they behaved the way they did. A look at history will help to explain this. The church was born under the rule of what was then the largest political empire in the known world, and that was Rome. Roman power conquered the areas of Greece, Western and most of Eastern Europe, Asia Minor (Turkey) and the northern coast of Africa. This also included the Middle East up to what would be the borders of Arabia. The Jewish people, up to 63 B.C., had been independent, having broken free from the Seleucid Dynasty and the mad king Antiochus Epiphanes, whose rule was prophesied by Daniel in Chapter 8, verse 9-14. The revolt of the Maccabees in 163 B.C. and the cleansing of the Temple by Judas Maccabeus brought about an independent Jewish rule under the Hasmoneans. That rule ended when the Roman general Pompey invaded Judea and conquered it for Rome. History tells us that Pompey entered the Holy of Holies and finding nothing, dismissed the role of God in the lives of the Judeans.

The Roman Empire began under the rule of Gaius Octavius Caesar, the adopted nephew of Julius Caesar, the dictator of the Roman Republic who was assassinated on March 15, 44B.C. Octavian laid low while a struggle for power was initiated by the foes of Caesar. In 31 B.C., Octavian led a group of soldiers and sailors to defeat the armies of his rival Mark Anthony and his cohort Cleopatra, the last pharaoh of the Ptolemaic Dynasty. This was the battle of Actium, and it brought a victory for Octavian. Anthony was killed and Cleopatra committed suicide, putting Egypt under Roman rule. Four years later, the Roman Senate made Octavian emperor of Rome, giving him the name Augustus, meaning "divine". He was an effective ruler who reformed the government and kept the peace of the empire. He is mentioned by Luke in the birth narrative of the Lord Jesus (Luke 2:1). Rome was a mix of polytheism (belief in many gods and goddesses). The beginnings of emperor worship began shortly after Augustus became ruler. Within this mix of paganism there was also the Roman-appointed " king of Judea" Herod whom history refers to as "the Great" for his massive building projects that included the Temple at Jerusalem, which began renovations in 20 B.C. and was not finished until 66 A.D., four years before its destruction

Herod was a cruel, despotic ruler who kept his throne by intrigue and suspicion. He had two of his sons killed for allegedly trying to usurp the throne and had his favorite wife killed, which he later regretted and had her body preserved so he could talk to it at night. Knowing that his power could be taken away by an act of the emperor and senate of Rome, he kept in good relations with the procurators, Roman governors, and the garrisons stationed in Judea. It is this Herod, who, in the last years of his rule, sought to eliminate the Christ child by ordering the killing of all babies under the age of two. This occurred in 4 B.C., making Jesus's birth around 6 B.C., affirming the historical record of Luke 2:2. Matthew's gospel states that Joseph took Mary and the baby to Egypt for safety. After Herod died and with his sons receiving portions of his kingdom did the family return to Judea, settling in the region of Galilee in the town of Nazareth. Luke 2 tells us that Jesus grew up "in favor with God and man." Nowhere in Scripture or the writings of the early church fathers (100 -400 A.D.) do we read of Jesus performing any signs, wonders, or miracles prior to his baptism by John. Any attempt to comment on these "silent" years between His birth and start of His public ministry is futile.

The Romans had decided to allow some self-autonomy to the Jews and let them continue their worship of God without interference. The spiritual leadership of the people rested with a group known as the Pharisees, a word meaning "the separated ones". These men, numbering around 6,000, were known for their piety and adherence to the Scriptures, in particular the Law of Moses. Over the years, they had written and practiced self-governing rules that defined how the people should live, particularly in regard to the Sabbath. By the time Jesus appeared on the scene, the rules overruled the truths of the Scriptures and the Pharisee's actions were now displayed as self- serving and reeked of adherence to legalities, but not to the LORD.

All throughout the gospels Jesus rebukes them for their hypocrisy and condemning them to hell for their actions (Matthew 23). These actions did not change their minds or their hearts. Instead, they plotted to kill the

LORD and they got the help of Rome to do it. This does not make the Jewish people the killers of Christ, nor was it the exclusive idea of Rome. As preachers have said throughout church history, our sins and the plan of God put Jesus on the cross as payment for our sins. By performing miracles and affirming not just His sacrifice for our sins, but also proving His claim to Be God Incarnate by His resurrection from the dead (Mark 14:61-62; John 2:19-21; Matthew 12:39-40; Luke 24:26-27; 1 Corinthians 15), the Lord Jesus proved and affirmed that He was the greatest apologist for the faith.

His death and resurrection has been proven in the prophecies written of Him in the Scriptures, by the eyewitness testimony of the apostles (John 20:28-31; Acts 1:1-4; 1 Corinthians 15:1-8), the recording of the Scripture copies by the church fathers, many of whom knew the apostles, the work of faithful researchers, Bible scholars, laity, and the testimony of millions who have come to Him for forgiveness of sins and the gift of eternal life. For the first few years of the early church, Rome left the followers of Jesus pretty much alone because they saw Christianity as an offshoot of Judaism. The Jewish authorities, however, saw the early church as a threat to their established order.

 The preaching of Peter on Pentecost had reminded them of what they had done to Jesus and yet offered them forgiveness for sins and a new life in Christ if they would repent. Peter's preaching cut to the heart of 3,000 Jews that Pentecost day and the church multiplied into the tens of thousands, seeing the conversions of both Jew and Gentile into the kingdom of God. Paul's conversion is presented to skeptics as proof of the resurrection. His zeal for Christ led to the gospel being presented not just in Asia Minor and the Middle East, but to Europe as well. By the end of the book of Acts, Christianity had spread to Rome itself.

The first sign of trouble for the church from Rome is written in Acts 18:2, when the edict of the emperor Claudius called for the banishment of the Jews from Rome for allegedly stirring up trouble because of a new belief, later to be the beginnings of Christianity in the city. The fact of persecution looms large in Acts, but we need to remember that this was to be the price of confessing Christ and walking in His ways (Matthew 24:9-14; Mark 139-13; Luke 21:12-19). Paul wrote of it (2 Timothy 3:12) as well as Peter, who was in the midst of the persecution brought about by the mad emperor Nero, who had been a conspirator in the murder of Claudius in 54 A.D. (1

Peter2:20; 3:14; 4:16; 5:10) What accusations were brought about by the Roman government against the Christians?

First, the Christians were considered atheists because they did not worship the various gods of the empire. They honored Caesar (Romans 13:1-8) but denied he was lord over all things and people. The Christians rightly believed that Jesus was Lord, and Rome considered that an act of sedition. Second, the Christians were mostly slaves, which, to the Romans was degrading and brought about a fear from the masters that they would revolt, calling Jesus their Master in all things and thus perceived by the Roman populace as an act of betrayal. Paul had referred in his letter to "those in Caesar's household" (Philippians 4:22).

Third, the worship services of the Christians were believed by Roman society to be an orgy of flesh-eating and blood-drinking, a reference to communion and fellowship of believers. Societal interpretation of communion was based upon what Jesus had said in His teachings (John 6:51-58). Although John's gospel had not been written yet, the apostle repeated these words as he taught in areas like Ephesus and Asia Minor. Apostolic travels brought this teaching to those who would believe. Paul makes mention of the proper partaking of communion in 1 Corinthians 11:23-26. It is certain that the Christians would have explained this to the misinformed hearer, possibly at the risk of their own lives.

Any explanations or defenses of belief were put to the test as Christians received the blame for setting fire to the city of Rome in 64 A.D. The fire was allegedly set by Nero, who wanted to build a new city and extravagant palace for himself. The citizens of Rome, who were rendered homeless and injured by the catastrophe, suspected and started to blame Nero. Desperate to avoid this accusation, he turned his fury towards the misunderstood and suspicious believers, who would undergo sheer terror as many were burned to death, crucified, torn apart by wild beasts in the Coliseum, and other horrid forms of torture. Peter and Paul met their demise by crucifixion and beheading respectively (2 Timothy 4:6-8; 2 Peter 1:12-15). As the persecutions continued, faithful believers got the word out, wrote defenses of the faith to magistrates and emperors, stayed steadfast, and their descendants carried the Gospel message to the ends of the world.

To live for Christ in any era of history means misunderstanding, hostility, ridicule, hatred, and sometimes the loss of life, as we have seen in this century. Still, we need to be prepared to give a defense of what and why we believe. It is part of the Great Commission and a part of growth as a believer. It is sound theology and as we progress in this book, we will look at the fulfillment of prophecy from a historical perspective and give you some spiritual ammunition to use when you witness or come across someone who, out of ignorance or errant speculation, needs to be shown the truths of the gospel.

Chapter 5
Surveying the Work of the Old Testament Prophets

It would be in our best interests to examine the Old Testament prophets and their work. We will not be able to concentrate on every one of them, but it is helpful to the prophecy student to know what each presented to the biblical narrative. As we progress further, we will look at prophecies such as the Messianic writings, the sagas of Psalm 83 and Isaiah Chapter 53, the drama of the Gog-Magog War of Ezekiel 38 and 39, and the visions of Daniel in Chapters 2, 7, and 9. Attention will be given to the nations involved, such as their history in relation to Israel and their respective fates.

Halley's Bible Handbook (1) with its notes, describe the prophets and the prophecies of the Messiah, who is the center of all the writings.

Isaiah

He was called the Messianic prophet because he was so thoroughly absorbed with the idea that his nation was to be the Messianic nation to the world, that is, a nation through whom one day a great and wonderful blessing would come from God to all nations, and he was continually dreaming of the day when that great and wonderful work would be done. The New Testament says that Isaiah "saw the glory of Christ and spoke of Him" (John 12:41). His time of writing was around 681 B.C.

Jeremiah

He was called to the prophetic office even before he was born (Jeremiah 1:5). He lived during the time of the rise of spiritual apostasy in the kingdom of Judah. He witnessed the gradual destruction of the kingdom by the Babylonians over a twenty- year period. Despite his preaching and call for the nation to repent, it came to naught. Jeremiah was ready to quit, but the call was too strong (20:9). He was a lonely man who had no converts and lived to see the kingdom fall in 586 B.C.

Ezekiel

He was a contemporary of Daniel in Babylon and may have been a pupil of Jeremiah. His ministry was to the exiles in Babylon. His mission seems to have been to explain the action of God in causing or permitting Israel's captivity. They had been guilty of the worst kind of idolatry. The captivity cured the years of idolatry once and for all. Ezekiel had a prophecy of Israel rising again to nationhood (Chapter 37), an end time war that would involve Israel and her foes, and the new temple of God (40-48).

Daniel

He was the statesman-prophet of both Babylon and Persia. He was taken to Babylon as a youth and gained favor with Nebuchadnezzar the king. He prophesied the rise and fall of kingdoms, the insanity of Nebuchadnezzar, the downfall of Babylon and the rise of Cyrus and Darius of Persia. He saw visions of the end times that have been and will be fulfilled (530 B.C.)

Hosea

This book was written around 715 B.C., recording the events of his ministry. He is known for marrying a harlot, representing faithless Israel and God's love for the nation despite her sins. This was written primarily for the inhabitants of the apostate kingdom of Israel which had embraced idolatry. It was a call of God to repent and return to Him.

Joel

The date of writing this prophecy is not known. There is little information on the prophet himself. He writes to the kingdom of Judah, telling of a plague of locusts and a severe drought regarded as punishments for the sins of the people. However, there is also a promise of the Spirit's outpouring upon the people in the latter days (2:28-32), a prophecy Peter quote to the people assembled on the day of Pentecost, resulting in 3,000 being saved (Acts 2:14-21, 41).

Amos

The name Amos means "burden". He was a citizen of Tekoa in the tribe of Judah. He was a herdsman and grower of figs. He prophesied around the years 755-750 B.C. during the reigns of Jeroboam II in Israel and Uzziah in Judah. The purpose of the prophecy was to pronounce God's righteous judgment upon His unrighteous people.

Obadiah

The prophet and the time of writing is not really known. The purpose of the book was to prophesy the doom of the Edomites because of their cruelty towards Judah and to reveal God's faithfulness to His own people and to His covenant promises.

Jonah

The prophet was probably the author of this drama. It was written anywhere between 783-753 B.B. during the reign of jeroboam II of Israel. The purpose for writing this is to reveal that salvation is of the LORD and that salvation extends to any who will repent and turn to Him, even the Gentiles.

Micah

Micah was a native of Judah. He prophesied during the reigns of Jotham, Ahaz, and Hezekiah. He was a contemporary of Isaiah. He spoke to both kingdoms, Israel and Judah. His book was written to warn God's people of the coming judgment for sin and to offer hope based upon God's mercy. The events occurred between 739 and 686 B.C.

Nahum

This oracle was written before the fall of Nineveh (612 B.C.) and the fall of the Egyptian city Thebes. Some scholars see this work as a sequel to Jonah. The Assyrians, who had been given mercy by God_relapsed into gross idolatry. This text prophesied divine vengeance and consolation for suffering Judah.

Habakkuk

He lived during the time of the Babylonian invasions (606-586 B.C.). It was written to remind the prophet that the God of Israel is the true God who is in control of everything and every event. He can be trusted amidst alleged calamity and uncertainty when all seems lost. The theme is the mysteries of Providence.

Zephaniah

He was a direct descendant of King Hezekiah (1:1). He prophesied during the reign of good king Josiah. This book was written around 640 B.C., the time of the religious revival. He motivated the people to repent and turn to God.

Haggai

He was born during the seventy years of exile and was a colleague of Zachariah. It was written around 520 B.C., during a period where the remnant that had returned were selfishly preoccupied with their own affairs to the detriment of the unfinished Temple. He told the remnant to reorder their priorities and restore proper worship, thus getting God's blessings.

Zechariah

He joined Haggai in arousing the Jews to rebuild the Temple. He wrote between 520-519 B.C. and the purpose was to give hope to God's people during a time when circumstances were trying and to promote spiritual revival in order to turn back to God.

Malachi

This book was written around 430 B.C. It was a message of confrontation to God's people and their leaders with their sins and plead with them to return to holiness. God will be the judge in all matters. Great reforms were needed to prepare the people for their coming Messiah.

The primary message of prophecy is for both individuals and nations to repent of sin and to prepare hearts for the One who will come and make all things new. When Jesus walked and talked with the travelers on the road to Emmaus, He opened their eyes to the prophecies concerning Him, beginning with Moses (Luke 24:13-35). We have looked at a handful of these prophecies in a previous chapter. Attention needs to be given to other prophetic messages about the Promised One. Below is a list of prophecies made and fulfilled by the Messiah, who is our Lord Jesus Christ, who came to deliver us from sin and separation from a holy God.

The Messiah would be the Seed of a woman (Genesis 3:15; Galatians 4:4), and the promised seed of Abraham, presented in Genesis 18:18 and proclaimed by the apostles in Acts 3:25. The Messiah would be the seed of Isaac. This is confirmed in Matthew 1:2 and is the promised seed of Jacob. This was a prophecy of Balaam (Numbers 24:17) and preserved in Luke's genealogy tracing Jesus' lineage back to Mary (Luke 3:34) He would be a direct descendant of Judah with the promise that royalty would come forth from him (Genesis 49:10). We turn to Luke's record as verification of this word (Luke 3:33)

He (the Messiah) would be the heir to the throne of David (Isaiah 9:7) and His royal bloodline would be confirmed by Matthew (1:1). His place of birth would be in David's birthplace, namely Bethlehem (Micah 5:2) and verified by Matthew 2:1. Daniel wrote of the time of the Messiah, given by the angel Gabriel from God, called the "Ancient of Days" (Daniel 7:9-10). The time was recorded in 9:25-26 and verified by Luke 2:1-2. The prophetic mission of Daniel and his vision will be the subject of study later in this volume.

He would be born of a virgin. This sign came from the prophet Isaiah (7:14) as a rebuke towards wicked king Ahaz's refusal to consult with the LORD. The prophecy was fulfilled in Mary (Matthew 1:18) and her submission to God's direction (Luke 1:30-35).Shortly after Jesus was born, Herod, fearing for the security of his Roman-appointed throne, ordered that all male infants under the age of two should be killed, an insane and evil attempt to kill the Promised One of God (Jeremiah 31:15; Matthew 2:18). HIs foster father Joseph was warned in a dream to take Him and His mother to Egypt, where they lived until Herod and all who wanted Jesus dead themselves died off (Hosea 11:1; Matthew 2:14).

The Messiah's ministry was to be in the region of Galilee, northwest of the Sea of Galilee (Isaiah 9:1-2, 42:6-7; Matthew 4:12-16). He would be the Prophet mentioned by Moses (Deuteronomy 18:15, 34:10; Luke 24:19; Acts 3:22; Hebrews 3:2).Though He was eagerly anticipated, the Messiah would, in the end, be rejected by His people (Isaiah 53:3; John 1:11). He would enter Jerusalem riding on a lowly animal, and for a brief time, be welcome with adulation from the crowds (Zechariah9:9; John 12:13-14)He would be betrayed by someone considered to be his friend (Psalm 41:9). This was fulfilled by the treacherous act of Judas Iscariot, who sold Jesus out for thirty pieces of silver, the price of a slave (Mark 14:10; Zechariah 11:12; Matthew 26:15). After his act of betrayal, Judas felt remorse, but not repentant as he returned the money. Afterwards, he went and hung himself, forever doomed. The money was used to buy a graveyard for the destitute (Zechariah 11:13; Matthew 27:6-7).

David prophesied that the Anointed One would have false accusations brought before Him (Psalm 27:12), fulfilled on the night of Jesus' illegal trial (Matthew 26:60-61). The Messiah would remain silent before His accusers (Isaiah 53:7). Jesus remained silent before people who would not listen to Him anyway (Matthew 26:62-63). He would be beaten and spat upon by the hands of an angry mob (Isaiah 50:6; Mark 14:65) and hated for no reason. The mentality towards Jesus as He headed to Calvary was one of blind, unsubstantiated rage. It served no purpose except to rally the crowd behind the cause of wanting to watch a Man die (Psalm 69:4; John 15:23-25)

The Messiah would face anger, persecution, misunderstanding, hatred, and ultimately death (Isaiah 53:4-5; Matthew 8:16-17), being in the company of those who would also die. This was fulfilled when our Lord was crucified and placed between two malcontents, one of whom trusted in the Lord and was ushered into Paradise (Isaiah 53:12; Luke 23:39-43; Matthew 27:38) The hands and feet of God's Anointed One would be pierced. David prophesied this in Psalm 22: 6-8 and would be fulfilled 1000 years later when Jesus was pierced with nails on the cross (John 20:27). Even during obvious injustice and blind hatred, God's Messiah would not bow to retribution, but instead pray for His enemies (Psalm 109:4; Luke 23:34) in dying, He was to be buried with the rich (Isaiah 53:9; Matthew 27:57-60) for He has no burial place of His own. The victory, however, is in the fact that He rose from the dead (Psalm 19:10; Matthew 28:9; Luke 24:36-48) and has ascended into heaven (Psalm 68:18; Luke 24:50-58).

For anyone to fulfill even five of these prophecies is equivalent to filling the state of Texas with quarters a foot deep, marking one with a red "x" and throwing it into the pile and being able to find it the first time. No one else in history could have fulfilled these prophecies except the Lord Jesus. There has never in the annals of history been anyone who was sinless, yet became sin for us, forever reconciling us with God, who had this all planned before anything was ever made. This says something about God's sovereignty. Nothing catches Him off guard or surprises Him. The crucifixion of Jesus Christ was not a plan that came up at the last moment. The plan of salvation was not a day-by-day affair to see what would happen next and hope that everything would fall into place. To think this way is an insult to the thoughts of God and his plans for redeeming fallen humanity. The God we serve does not foresee things and then puts everything into action. He knew from the foundation of the world that we would fall due to our free will and the wiles of the enemy.

We have to remember something, and that is even the enemy is a tool in God's hand for redemption because he is shown to be a defeated foe due to Christ's victory on the cross, and over death, hell, and the grave. The devil is only going to work in this world for a short time and his words and actions are limited by God. He does not have free reign. We are not to let the devil tell us that we are too bad to be saved. That is a hell-produced lie. Because of Christ's triumphant mission, we have the gift of eternal life and a home with Him. That act of love on the cross settles the issue of God's love for us. The beauty of prophecy is that we are given access not only to the redemptive plan of Almighty God, but an absolute certainty that the evils we face as believers and in the world will come to an end. Now let us look at representative prophecies that present victorious outcomes for God's people in the end times.

Chapter 6
The Fifth Gospel of Isaiah

When you ask a Christian, whether a long-time believer or a novice, about the subject of prophecy, probably the first thing that comes to mind are the events leading up to the Second Coming of Jesus Christ. Much prophetic scholarship has focused on this area. To know the possible sequence of end-time events gets us excited for the possibility that Jesus may come in our lifetime and set up His kingdom here on Earth. A lot of ink and thought have been used to come up with the varied theories of how everything in history could come to a grand climax, with Jesus at the center of it all.

Much attention has been given to the future, and rightly so. However, we may be missing something that is just as relevant in the prophetic discourse, and it is not dealing with issues such as the timing of the Rapture, the Tribulation, pre, post, or no millennium at all. It should rightly focus on the mission and person of Jesus Christ. Without Him as the center, everything about Bible prophecy would be a waste of time and effort. The focus should always be on Him, not figuring out which leader would be the best candidate for the Antichrist. According to a majority of prophecy experts, the Christians will be taken out of the coming troubles (John 14:1-3; 1 Thessalonians 4:13-18; 1 Corinthians 15:51-58) through the event known as the Rapture of the church, which will be presented in more detail later. The remainder of the chapter will focus on an analysis of the prophecies of Isaiah concerning the person and mission of the Promised Messiah and His work of redemption for the sins of the people. We start with a study of the prophet himself.

The name Isaiah means "Yahweh Saves". It is an appropriate name for the prophet who, in his writing, tells of not only that God is a God of judgment, but also of mercy and salvation. The Holman Bible Dictionary (1) records that the prophet was active in the kingdom of Judah from 740 – 701. His ministry spanned from his call (741 B.C.) until the last years of King Hezekiah (716-687 B.C.) or the early years of Manasseh (687-642 B.C.) He lived through the reigns of Uzziah, Jotham, Ahaz, and Hezekiah, and gave advice to all of them. He also knew the last four wicked kings of Israel and the prophesied fall of the Northern Kingdom of Israel in 722 B.C. He was born in Jerusalem about 760 B.C., had a knowledge of the religious systems of both Israel and Judah and was a highly educated man with both a knowledge of history and the political landscape.

He was married, although we do not know the name of his wife. He had two sons, one of them being named Maher-shalal-hash –Baz, so named because before he would be old enough to talk, the threats against Judah by the nation of Assyria would be gone. The naming of this child occurred after Isaiah prophesied to the unbelieving King Ahaz that a virgin would conceive and bear a son with the name of Immanuel, meaning "God with us" (Isaiah 7:14). There are key events in the book that merit our attention before we get to analyzing what many scholars have called "the fifth Gospel", namely, Isaiah 52:13-53:12. We start with an observation made in Chapter 5, verses 20 -21.

"Woe to those who call evil good, and good evil; who substitute darkens for light and light for darkness; who substitute bitter for sweet, and sweet for bitter! Woe to those who are wise in their own eyes and clever in their own sight! (NASB)

The prophet is describing the attitude of the individual or nation that has adopted the view of a world without the direction of God, and adopting an attitude of relativism, the thought that whatever is true for someone may not be true for another. There is, in effect, no absolute standard by which we can decide if something is right or wrong. They have adopted the attitude of the Israelites in Judges 21:25: *"In those days there was no king; everybody did what was right in their own eyes."* This is a dangerous attitude to have as a person and in a nation. When there is no standard, especially as determined by God, there is nothing but a mindless quagmire of various thoughts and theories that do not help anyone or give adequate solutions to problems. Good and evil are what one makes of it.

People in a relativistic mind set have no clear direction for their lives, nor do they want to in most cases because to have an absolute standard conflicts with their choice of lifestyle or attitude that they have adopted to suit their own tastes and viewpoint. Whenever a person who is transformed by the power of God reads Scripture and lives by the dictates of Christ's example and teachings, it flies in the face of a world that is comfortable with their own morality, which according to God, may be totally degrading and immoral leading to eternal consequences. The cure for relativistic thinking is a clear presentation of the Gospel and prayer for wisdom and guidance in approaching people. Not everyone is totally entrenched in degradation. There are a lot of people who search for meaning and purpose, but always in the wrong places. Jesus told His disciples to be salt and light in order to make people thirsty for His living water and a light in the midst of spiritual darkness.

We now come to the episode in Isaiah's life where he was called by God into the prophetic ministry (Isaiah 6:1-8): "*In the year of King Uzziah's death, I saw the LORD sitting on a throne, lofty and exalted, with the train of His robe filling the temple. Seraphim stood above Him, each having six wings; with two he covered his face, and with two he covered his feet, and with two he flew. And one called out to another, and said: 'HOLY, HOLY, HOLY is the LORD of Hosts; the whole earth is full of HIs glory.' And the foundations of the thresholds trembled at the voice of him who called ut while the temple was filled with smoke. Then I said, 'Woe is me, for I am ruined! Because I am a man of unclean lips, and I live among a people of unclean lips; for my eyes have seen the KING, the LORD of Hosts!' Then one of the seraphim flew to me, with a burning coal in his hand which he had taken from the altar with tongs. And he touched my mouth with it and said, 'Behold, this has touched your lips, and your iniquity is taken away, and your sin is forgiven.' Then Is heard the voice of the LORD saying, "Whom shall I send, and who will go for us?' Then I said, 'Here am I. Send me."* (NASB)

Note the solemnity of the encounter. Isaiah is in the Temple in the act of worship when he gets a vision of the LORD in a demonstration of His absolute holiness. The seraphim (angelic beings) do not look upon the face of the LORD because He is perfection and is glorious. No one can look upon Him and live. He abhors any sin in His presence. God is to be feared. We should be scared, being as we are. We have too casual an attitude of God in the modern church. There is a relaxed attitude towards God's character and nature today, and that is not how it should be, considering we are talking about the very ONE who spoke all things into existence (Colossians 1:16; Genesis 1:1) and holds our very lives in His hand, which He can take away at His pleasure.

It is an arrogant individual who thinks that he has everything under control in his life. Without God, we are nothing. Isaiah is terrified and believes he is doomed for even getting a glance at the LORD while in his current sinful state. The mercy of the LORD is presented here as well as His majesty. The angelic being takes a white-hot coal and presses it against the lips of Isaiah. This represents the pain of sin and its devastating effect on the spiritual character of him and all who encounter God. Through prayer and interaction with Him through the reading of the Word, the exhortation of godly preachers and teachers, or even in the quiet of one's own home, His presence is unmistakable. In this dispensation, we now have access to God through the finished work of Jesus Christ on the cross as payment for our sins. Jesus is our intercessor, according to the book of Hebrews, and because of Jesus, nothing can separate us from His love (Romans 8:31-39).

After the purging and declaration of cleanliness, God now asks a question. Who will take up the task of proclaiming His truth to the nation? Without hesitation, Isaiah offers himself to be God's spokesman. His encounter with the living God has transformed him into a vehicle for service. This is a definite calling into godly service. The office of pastor/teacher, the modern equivalent of a prophet, is not some career choice because one has nothing better to do but is a sacred honor not to be taken lightly. When a man is called of God into service, He expects that man to prepare himself by daily communion in prayer, times of diligent study, teaching the Word, and to keep a good testimony. A man of God should have the qualifications as presented in 1 Timothy 3:1-8. He should prepare himself by getting the best education possible. God does not just put knowledge of Himself into the person's head. He is to use his mind as well as his spirit in rightly dividing the word of truth. It is an honor and privilege to serve the LORD in whatever capacity He has called you. We are all ministers of the truth with different gifts to use for His service (1 Corinthians 12:6-11) and are not to squander the gifts that God has given us, as we will be all held accountable to the LORD for the service we rendered Him (2 Corinthians 5:10).

Isaiah's writings contain numerous references to the rule and person of God's Messiah. There are two specific passages that are of interest. One deals with His rule as King, and the other deals with the world that He shall rule. In Isaiah 9:6-7, we read:

For a child will be born to us, a Son will be given to us; and the government will rest on His shoulders. And His name will be called Wonderful Counselor, Mighty God, Eternal Father, Prince of Peace. There will be no end to the increase of His government or of peace, on the throne of David and over His kingdom, to establish it and to uphold it with justice and righteousness from then on and forevermore. The zeal of the LORD of Hosts will accomplish this." (NASB)

Here we see the mission of none other than the Lord Jesus Christ. This passage is a praiseworthy summary of the LORD's redemptive work. The first part of verse 6 refers to His First Advent. His first coming is foretold, yet He was not born to an earthly monarch in a palace. His birth was not heralded by Caesar or Herod, nor viewed as special in the eyes of the world. The heavenly host instead announced His birth to the lowest group within that society, a group of shepherds with no standing among the elites of the world(Luke 2: 8-18) but were still chosen as the first messengers of the Savior's birth to the people, who, according to Luke's investigation, merely "wondered".

The ones to whom the good news was told really did nothing. Even now, it is an accurate description of people's attitudes today when they are presented with the Gospel. The rest of verse 6 tells of the LORD's eternal rule. He is bestowed with many names which describe His character and personality as King. He is our wonderful counselor who has born our sorrows and burdens and can understand us. He is the Mighty God, creator and sustainer of life and all that there is in the universe. No one is His equal. He is Sovereign in all the affairs of creation. He is all powerful, all wise, all loving, and brings all things under His eternal rule. There will be no more war, no more conflict, no more hatred, no more division, no more despotism, no evil, no devil, and no more strife to tear us apart. His government will be one of justice and love, emitting from the righteous throne of Christ's ancestor David. His zeal for the things of God will be made manifest throughout eternity. Those of us who are in Christ will rule and reign with Him for eternity, heirs of riches the world cannot even begin to contain.

We will have new, incorruptible bodies that will never see death or pain. We will be free from the oppression that many of us have had to endure on this earth. There will be a new heaven and a new earth (Revelation 21, 22) for us to enjoy and best of all, we will be with our LORD forever to love and praise Him and to enjoy eternal life with our loved ones. That is what it means to be ruled by the great King who Isaiah saw in his prophetic vision. The reality of a glorious eternal kingdom ruled by the Messiah is found in just after Chapter 10, which describes the deliverance of Israel from the hands of the Assyrians. A fallible, earthly monarch can only do so much for his people, and most of the kings of that day relied more on their own intellect and strategy than they did on the LORD. The kings of Israel and Judah reflect this observation.

The beginning of the eleventh chapter tells of a future time when the era of kings was done, and it seems that there is no hope of them ever coming back. Yet, God is not done with the idea of a monarch. Earthly kings are only temporal, but God will place upon the throne of David an eternal king.

God's Messiah and Righteous One will rule over an Earth dwelling in peace, a scene joyfully described in Isaiah11: 1-9:

"Then a shoot shall spring from the stem of Jesse, and a Branch from his roots will bear fruit, and the Spirit of the LORD will rest on Him, the spirit of wisdom and understanding, the spirit of counsel and strength, the spirit of knowledge and the fear of the LORD. He will delight in the fear of the LORD, and He will not judge by what HIs eyes see, nor make a decision by what His ears hear. But with righteousness He will judge the poor and decide with fairness for the afflicted of the earth, and He will strike the earth with the rod of his mouth, and with the breath of His lips He will slay the wicked."

"Also righteousness will be the belt around His loins, and faithfulness the belt about His waist. And the wolf will dwell with the lamb, and the leopard will lie down with the kid; and the calf and the young lion and the fatling together; and a little will shall lead them. The cow and the bear will graze; their young will lie down together; and the lion will eat straw like the ox. The nursing child will play by the hole of the cobra, and the weaned child will put his hand on the viper's den. They will not hurt or destroy in all My holy mountain; for the earth will be full of the knowledge of the LORD as the waters cover the sea."(NASB)

Isaiah wrote his prophecies while there were two kingdoms claiming descent from God. There was the northern kingdom of Israel, which had abandoned the worship of the true God in order to serve idols and fall further into apostasy. No king of Israel pointed the people to the true God and the situation worsened under the rule of the wicked duo Ahab and Jezebel, who transformed Israel into a center of Phoenician deity worship, in particular Baal the fertility god, of whose priests Elijah had fought against and won as God proved Himself to be true. In 1 Kings 18:20-40, Elijah had the priests of Baal put to death for leading the people into gross idolatry. It would not be so far in the future that terrible deaths came to Ahab and Jezebel as well. Most of the kings of Israel got to the throne because of murder and intrigue. It was in decline by the time Isaiah began his ministry and fell to Assyrian control and exile in 722 B.C.

Judah still had the Davidic lineage and there was a continual line of rulers who had ascended to the throne due to bloodline. However, Judah had a mix of godly and ungodly kings who led the people into idol worship and the desecration of the Temple. The king who had done much for Judah and who died when Isaiah began his ministry was Uzziah. His rule brought prosperity to the nation, and he was a God-fearing ruler who reigned for fifty-two years (2 Kings 15:1-7; 2 Chronicles 26:22-23). His son Jotham was also devoted to God (2 Kings 15:32-38; 2 Chronicles 27:1-9), but really did not do much in the way of strengthening Judah's faith. Jotham's son Ahaz (2 Kings 16:1-20; 2 Chronicles 28:1-27)was a wicked king who offered his children as a sacrifice to the perverse god Moloch as well as form unreliable alliances with pagan rulers. After his reign came good king Hezekiah (2 Kings 18:1-20:21; 2 Chronicles 29:1-32:33), who brought the people back to God and witnessed the defeat of the invading Assyrians through a supernatural act of the LORD. God spared his life when he was at the point of death and gave him fifteen additional years. It was during that time, however, that he became the father of Judah's worst ruler, the wicked and perverse king Manasseh, who according to tradition, had Isaiah sawn in two.

Judah had one final godly ruler in the notable and righteous reign of Josiah (2 Kings 22:1-23:30; 2 Chronicles 34:1-35:27), who initiated major reforms and dedicated himself to the things of God. After his death, the kingdom grew weaker and weaker with a succession of ungodly rulers. The apostate kingdom of Judah fell to the Babylonians in 586 B.C., and Israel has not had a king since then. The passage describes a root from out of the stump of Jesse, which symbolized that the kingdom of David was finished with no chance of resurrecting it in the earthly realm.

A stump is what is left of a tree or bush that had been fruitful and productive. Now there is nothing. Yet, God still has a use for it. A Branch shall grow out of it, representing the rule of the coming Messiah. The Spirit of the LORD will be upon this branch, and He will be given wisdom, knowledge, the ability to bring forth sound counsel, He will not allow His emotions to be the deciding factor in the hearing of cases but will judge fairly and with the compassion of the LORD. When we look at these verses, there is no doubt that this is a reference to the work and person of the Lord Jesus Christ. He grew up in a state of anonymity with no visible heritage or wealth. He was reared in an obscure village off the beaten path.

His teachings were extraordinary and drew people to the love of God, but was cut down, meant to be forgotten by the world. He instead rose from the dead and was the enough payment or our sins. When He comes to take possession of this world, it will become like Eden. The animal kingdom will be at peace, with animosity a thing of the past. Children will be able to play with creatures that in this present world would kill them. Animals that tore each other apart for food now lie peacefully side by side, eating straw and

64

the plants of the field. All strife will disappear, and He will rule with justice, tranquility, and love forever in righteousness. This golden era was something that the Jewish people were anticipating. It will come to pass when Jesus Christ returns to this world to recreate and establish it.

We now turn our attention to the passage of Scripture referred to as "another gospel" by great men of God such as the Reformer John Calvin, the 19th century preachers Dwight L. Moody and Charles H. Spurgeon and is the view of Bible-believing theologians today like Dr. John MacArthur. It is one of the clearest pictures of the person and work of God's Servant, the Messiah. As stated in the name of this chapter, what we will now examine is considered the crown jewel of prophecy, namely Isaiah 52:13 - 53:12.

This section of Scripture was no doubt used by our LORD to teach the two disciples on the road to Emmaus (Luke 24:27) about why the Messiah had to die and how He fulfilled that requirement. It reads as follows:

"Behold, my Servant will prosper. He will be high and lifted up and be greatly exalted. Just as many were astonished at you, My people, so His appearance was marred more than any man, and His form more than the sons of men. Thus He will sprinkle many nations; kings will shut their mouths on account of Him; for what had not been told them they will see; and what they had not heard will they understand. Who has believed our message, and to whom has the arm of the LORD been revealed? For He grew up before Him like a tender shoot, and as a root out of parched ground. He has no stately form or majesty that we should look at Him, nor appearance that we should be attracted to Him. He was despised and forsaken of men; a man of sorrows and acquainted with grief, and like one from whom men hide their face. He was despised, and we did not esteem Him. Surely our griefs He Himself bore, and our sorrows He carried, yet we ourselves esteemed Him stricken, smitten of God and afflicted. But He was pierced through for our transgressions. He was crushed for our iniquities. The chastising for our well-being fell upon Him, and by His scourging we are healed".

"All of us like sheep have gone astray. Each of us has turned to his own way, but the LORD has caused the iniquity of us all to fall on Him. He was oppressed, and He was afflicted, yet He did not open His mouth, like a lamb that is led to the slaughter, and like sheep that is silent before his shearers, so He did not open His mouth. By oppression and judgment He was taken away, and as for His generation who considered. He was cut off from the land of the living for the transgression of My people to whom the stroke was due. His grave was assigned with wicked men, yet He was with a rich man in His death because he had done no violence, nor was any there any deceit in His mouth. But

the LORD was pleased to crush Him, putting Him to grief, if He would render Himself as a guilt offering, He will see His offspring, He will prolong His days, and the good pleasure of the LORD will prosper in His hand. As a result of the anguish of His soul, He will see it and be satisfied. By His knowledge the Righteous One, My servant, will justify the many, as He will bear their iniquities. Therefore I will allot Him a portion with the great, and He shall divide the spoil with the strong, because He poured out Himself to death, and was numbered with the transgressors, yet He Himself bore the sin of many, and interceded for the transgressors." (NASB)

Chapters 52 and 53 describe someone who is unique in the history of Israel. Attention now turns to the One called the Servant of Jehovah. These Scriptures describe the mission and ministry of One who will bear the sins of the people. These verses clearly describe the work of the Lord Jesus Christ. Chapter 52:13-15 and 53:1-12 are a complete narrative concerning the work of the Messiah. This passage has opened the eyes of many as the direct prophecy of who Jesus is and what He has done for us. It is worth carefully examining.

52:13-15: The Sin-Bearing Servant

The Glory that Will Be with the Servant (v.13) - He shall be prudent. He will deal with all things with order and stability. Nothing will escape His attention. The Messiah's reign will be exalted by all peoples under His eternal reign. His people will gladly obey Him in the eternal state. His majesty will be high in all aspects. He is the exalted King for all eternity. His time of rule and reign will come at His pleasure.

The Astonishing View of the Servant (v.14) - The sight of the Servant will astonish the people. No one will expect His looks to be less than wondrous. The Servant will be wounded to the point where He is unrecognizable. His appearance will be more marred than any other person on this globe. The Servant's looks will turn people away. It is the mission that is important.

The Work of the Servant in the Future (v.15) - The Servant's rule will be absolute over His elect nation. The rulers of the earth will be silent before Him, such is His majesty. The rulers will be witness to the glorifying work of God. The rulers will consider and meditate upon what has been revealed by the Servant. The rulers will be subject to the Servant, who is the Promised King of His people. These verses show the ultimate rule of the Lord Jesus Christ.

53:1-3: The Amazing Servant of Jehovah

With this chapter, we begin to see the mission and purpose of God's Messiah. An objective reader of these Scriptures will see that the One mentioned here describes no one else but the Lord Jesus Christ. It is this chapter that was read by the Ethiopian official and explained by the evangelist Phillip that led to the official's salvation (Acts 8:26-46). It is a witness both to Jew and Gentile. There are observations to be made in these beginning verses that detail what the Servant of Jehovah is like.

The Amazing News Is Rejected (v.1) - Isaiah asks who will believe what is stated here. It is a note of what Isaiah would face in his own prophetic mission (6:9-10) Jesus would prophesy about the consequences of not heeding His word (Matthew 23:38; Luke 10: 13-16) The nation's hardness of heart meant that others would hear the message (Acts 13:46-48)

The Amazing Appearance is Rejected (v.2) - The Servant comes from a line that is apparently dried up; namely the royal line of David (2 Samuel 7:16) He comes from a humble background. He wears nothing formal, nor does He look like a warrior King (John 1:43-51). He bears no beauty. He looks like an average man, with no outstanding characteristics (2 Corinthians 8:9; Philippians 2:7-8)

The Amazing attitude of the Nation (v.3) - The nation would despise and reject Him (Matthew 27:32-44) The Servant will be a Man of Sorrows and acquainted with grief. He identifies with the people (Hebrews 4:14-16; John 12:27, 35). The nation would turn its back on Him, despising and holding Him in low esteem. We see this throughout the ministry of Jesus (Mark 3:1-6; Matthew 16:1; 19:3) We see this as an apt description of the world in general (Matthew 13:15; Romans 1:28; 2 Peter 3:5) The consequences of rejection are horrid (Revelation 20:11-15)

53: 4-6: The Salvation Mission of the Servant

We get into the heart of why the Servant has come. It is a forerunner to the end of the sacrificial system that Israel has known for generations. His time will be a fulfillment of what is written in the words of another prophet (Jeremiah 31:31-34). His mission is one not just of sacrifice, but one of redemption for a rebellious people. These verses present this scene. This is a glorious passage describing the salvation of peoples from all around, and is a glorious mission designed to redeem the people of God.

The Burden of the Servant (v.4) - Isaiah presents the fact that God puts these burdens on the Servant. The Servant bears our griefs and sorrows

(Matthew 11:28-30) The people watch as He is stricken (Luke 23:16; Mark 15:16-30) God Himself strikes and afflicts the Servant (Psalm 22:1-2, 6-8, 16-18). The question is "Why"?

The Purpose of the Suffering Servant (v.5) - He is wounded for our transgressions (1 Corinthians 15:3; 2 Corinthians 5:21; Galatians 3:3; 1 Peter 3: 18) He is bruised for the sake of our iniquities His chastisement is for the sake of our eternal peace. We are healed spiritually because of His wounds and beatings.

The portrait of the Rebellious (v.6) - We are lost sheep without a shepherd (Jeremiah 50:6; Ezekiel 34:6; John 10:11). We all go our own direction with no one to guide us (1 Peter 2:25). God himself lays our sins upon His servant (Hebrews 9:28; 1 Peter 2:24; John 3:5). Christ, the Suffering Servant, came to die for our sins and rescue us from our iniquities. Let us give Him thanksgiving and praise for Hs love and compassion.

53:7-9: The Salvation Mission Continues

We are continuing our look at the redeeming work of God's servant, who is the Messiah, Jesus Christ. We have examined His purposes, His rejection by the people, His wounds and beating, and the fact that we are like lost sheep, not knowing our way and in need of a Shepherd.

The Servant's Peaceful Attitude (v.7) - His suffering was foreordained (Isaiah 50:6; Zechariah 13:6). He never opened His mouth to defend Himself (Isaiah 42:2; Matthew 26:62-63; 27:14; Mark 15:3; Luke 23:9). He is the Lamb of God (John 1:29-34)

The Servant's Judgment for sin (v.8) - He was judged by Pilate and found not guilty. He asked His enemies if they had ever seen Him sin (John 8:46). His death was for the transgressions of the people.

The Servant without Sin (v.9) - When He died, there was no place to bury Him. He was placed in a rich man's tomb. He was without vice or deceit (Luke 23:41; 2 Corinthians 5; 21). His work had been done.

53:10-12: The Victorious Servant of Jehovah

The mission of God's Servant is coming to a wonderful and glorious conclusion, being the redemption of people from their sins and transgressions. Isaiah concludes this section of his numerous prophecies with a declaration of the redemptive work of the servant being enough and glorifying to the LORD. The redeeming work of the Servant pleases God. No other sacrifices need to be done.

The Wondrous Reward of the Servant (v.10) - God is pleased with the Servant after he is bruised for our iniquities. This refers to the Atonement, which is the doctrine of the covering over and eradication of sin, which is accomplished through the work of Christ on the cross. The Servant will see the fruit of His labors (Hebrews 9:27-28; Revelation 7:9-10). His finished work is prosperous in that here is much fruit (1 Timothy 1:15-17).

The Finished Work of the Servant (v.11) - He will see his work prosper. The sacrifice bears good results (Acts 15:11; Romans 5:9). His sacrificial work brings salvation to many people (Ephesians 1:4; 1 Peter 1:1-2; Romans 9:15-16, 18.) He has born our iniquities so that we do not have to do so (2 Corinthians 5:21; Galatians 3:13; 1 Peter 3; 18).

The Just Reward of the Servant (v.12) - The Servant is victorious in His mission. The reward of redemption is to be shared with His people (1 Corinthians 15:24). He poured out His soul and died for us. He identified with transgressors. He bore our sins and interceded for us (Hebrews 4:14). No one else fits this description except the Lord Jesus Christ. Glory be to his name! Without the promises of Isaiah 53, other prophecies would simply make no sense. Now we turn our attention to God's chosen people and their place in history and the prophetic scenario.

Chapter 7
The Dry Bones of Israel in Ezekiel 37

We have looked at Jesus Christ, the center of all prophecy, and His mission. The bulk of prophecy focuses on Him and also the future of the nation of Israel. The Scriptures tell of Israel's unstable relationship with God in a series of rebuttals and condemnations for their unfaithfulness to God and His commandments. In the same Scriptures we also read about God's desire to see His people come to a state of repentance and renewal, but HIs pleas to return to Him or face the consequences often fell on deaf ears. Instead there was a turn to rampant idolatry and apostasy, and the children of Israel were daring God to do something about it.

Despite the words of His prophets and His personal intervention, little changed throughout Israel's troubled history. There were periods of reprieve during the reigns of godly kings such as David, Hezekiah, and Josiah. There were also periods of rank and defiant unbelief combined with a false formality of worship in the times of Ahaz and Manasseh. God had to do something to honor His name and word and allowed the kingdoms of Israel and Judah to fall into enemy hands as punishment for their deeds. Scripture devotes much attention to the fate of the residents of what had been the kingdom of Judah, which started to decline in 605 B.C., when the first wave of citizens were sent to Babylon under the direction of king Nebuchadnezzar, which was when the prophet Daniel was exiled to Babylon and began his time of service to Nebuchadnezzar. There will be more to say about the work of Daniel in later chapters. Attention needs to be given to another prophet in exile, specifically Ezekiel.

The prophet's ministry occurred during the early years of the Babylonian Exile, from approximately 593 – 570 B.C. His visions from God showed the fall and restoration of the people of Israel. His older contemporary, Jeremiah, saw the decline and fall of the kingdom of Judah in 586 B.C. We need to set up some historical backgrounds as to why Babylon became such a formidable power. In 605 B.C. the armies of Babylon under Nebuchadnezzar defeated the armies of the Egyptian Pharaoh Necho at the Battle of Carchemish on the Euphrates River in 605 B.C., securing Babylon as a major power on the world stage. They set up the kingdom of

Judah as a vassal state, meaning that Judah had to pay annual monetary tribute to them, with severe consequences if they dared to disobey.

After the death of the godly king Josiah, ironically at the hands of Necho, his descendants followed in the ways of their idolatrous ancestral kings, disregarding God and persecuting the prophets (Jeremiah 7: 26, 36). King Jehoiakim (608-597) degraded the spiritual life of the nation (Jeremiah 7:1-15) and proved to be a petty tyrant (Jeremiah 22:13-15). He foolishly rebelled against Nebuchadnezzar and soon died in disgrace before Nebuchadnezzar could get to him. The next ruler, Jehoiachin, ruled only three months and surrendered to Nebuchadnezzar (2 Kings 24:8-17; Jeremiah 22:24-30; Ezekiel 19:5-9). The Babylonian monarch then pillaged Jerusalem and took with him thousands of notable citizens back to Babylon. It was during this time that the prophet began his work among the people. Representative sections of Ezekiel are worth examining, starting with the enigmatic first chapter.

Ezekiel, like Isaiah before him, saw a portion of the glory of God and His angelic beings, who are at God's bidding. They are glorious creatures, with their appearance conveying God's immutable magnificence. The wheels represent the ongoing war machine of God as He exercises righteous judgment on a stubborn people. God's glory shines through. This is a theophany, a vision of the LORD, in particularly an image of the pre-incarnate Lord Jesus Christ. Ezekiel, upon seeing this, falls on his face in awe and wonder of what he has just witnessed. Here is where he receives his call as a prophet, receiving God's message to give to the people, who will prove to be stubborn and reluctant to hear it.

Ezekiel's responsibility as a prophet (Ezekiel 3: 17-21) serves as a warning to those whom God has entrusted with the spiritual well-being and care of the people: *"Son of man (a term used to describe the prophet), I have appointed you a watchman to the house of Israel. Whenever you hear a word from My mouth, warn them from Me. When I say unto the wicked, 'You shall surely die; and you do not warn him or speak out to warn the wicked from his wicked way that he may live, that wicked man shall die in his iniquity; but his blood will I require your hand. Yet if you have warned the wicked, and he does not turn from his wicked way, he shall die in his iniquity; but you have delivered yourself. When a righteous man turns from his righteousness and commits iniquity, and I place an obstacle before him, he shall die; because you have not warned him, he shall die in his sin, and his righteousness deeds which he has done shall not be remembered; but his blood will I require at your hand. However, if you have warned the righteous man that he should not sin, he shall surely live because he took warning, and you have delivered yourself." (NASB)*

This is a serious mandate to warn people about the LORD and the consequences of not obeying Him. There are people that we know and others we run across who are lost and without hope. We may be the one individual who comes into their life and can give them the fact that they are lost and will face God one day. If we do not tell them about the LORD. This is sound advice from God Himself to both pastor and people. Continuing the theme of warning and repentance, Ezekiel 18:21-23 presents the LORD's attitude towards the wicked who repent: *"But if the wicked turns from all his sins which he has committed, and observes all My statutes, and practices justice and righteousness, he shall surely live, he shall not die. All transgressions which he has committed shall not be remembered against him. Because of his righteousness that he has practiced, he will live. 'Do I have any pleasure in the death of the wicked', declares the LORD God, rather that he should turn from his ways, and live?" (NASB)*

God promises to punish the wicked if they do not turn from their wrongdoing. Yet even with this warning, there are many who will refuse to turn away from their wicked behavior. The New Testament also gives words of encouragement to those who seek peace with God: *"The LORD is not slow about His promise, as some count slowness, but is patient toward you, not wishing for any to perish, but for all to come to repentance." – 2 Peter 3:9 (NASB)*

The central theme of the Scriptures is the call from God to turn away from our sins and embrace the saving grace of the Lord Jesus Christ. Here is where God's sovereignty and man's responsibility comes to light. God is in control of people's salvation, and He can save whomever He wishes (Exodus 33:19; Romans 9:14-18). He has control and nothing takes Him by surprise. Yet, we are responsible for either embracing or rejecting His offer of salvation. There is no other option available (John 14:6). Salvation is freely offered to anyone (Matthew 11:28-30), yet so few take it (Romans 10:13). There are many who will simply not believe, and God is not wringing His hands over it.

When we look at the panorama of biblical history, we see a record of unfaithfulness on Israel's part. Yet, God is not finished with them, and He will make them the primary nation when the Lord Jesus comes back to rule and reign. Ezekiel 37:1-28 presents an episode in the life of Israel that describes the bleak picture of its past and the blessed promise of its future. Starting with Verses 1-14, we read: *"The hand of the LORD was upon me, and*

He brought me out by the spirit of the LORD and set me down in the middle of the valley, and it was full of bones. And He caused me to pass among them round about, and behold, there were very many on the surface of the valley; and, lo, they were very dry. And He said to me, Son of man, can these bones live? And I answered, O LORD GOD, Thou knowest."

"Again He said to me, 'Prophesy over these bones and say to them, 'O dry bones, hear the word of the LORD'. Thus says the LORD God to these bones, 'Behold, I will cause breath to enter you, that you may come to life.' And I will put sinews on you, make flesh go back on you, cover you with skin, and put breath in you, that you may come alive, and you will know that I am the LORD. So I prophesied as I was commanded, and as I prophesied, there was a noise, and behold, a rattling, and the bones came together, bone to his bone. And I looked, and behold, sinews were on them, and skin covered them: but there was no breath in them. Then He said to me, Prophesy to the breath, prophesy, son of man and say to the breath, 'Thus says the LORD GOD; come from the four winds, O breath, and breathe on these slain, that they come to life. So I prophesied as He commanded me, and the breath came into them, and they came to life, and stood on their feet, an exceedingly great army. Then He said to me, 'Son of man, these bones are the whole house of Israel; behold they say, 'Our bones are dried up, and our hope has perished. We are completely cut off'. Therefore prophesy and say to them, 'Thus says the LORD GOD, 'Behold! I will open your graves and cause you to come up out of your graves, Andi will bring you to the land of Israel. Then you shall know that I am the LORD, when I have opened your graves, and caused you to come up out of your graves, My people". And I will put My Spirit within you, and you will come to life, and I will place you on your own land. Then you will know that I, the LORD have spoken and done it, declares the LORD."(NASB)

When Ezekiel wrote this, the land of Israel had turned into a barren and desolate wasteland. The people had either been killed or exiled to Babylon. The kingdom was gone for good in their eyes and they would not know what it would be like to be back in the land for another seventy years. Walter Roehrs, writing in the <u>Biblical Expositor (1)</u> says this about Israel's situation:

"Israel's hopes for the future appeared dead and buried forever in the exile. Her prospects of revival were like a vast array of dead men's bones, lying dismembered and dry and dust in a great plain. Shall they live again? Yes, says God, by the power of His creative word. When Ezekiel speaks at God's command, the power of death vanishes. The bones arrange themselves according to their proper function and covered with sinews and flesh. Let not Israel doubt His power! But this demonstration of God's life-giving power contains assurance beyond the revival of Israel as a nation. The vision of the future shows

that Israel is an earthly clay out of which God will call into being the people of His eternal kingdom."

Some prophecy scholars tend to believe that this valley of dry bones represents the people of Israel after the horrors of the Holocaust, when the surviving Jews of Europe had nowhere to go and no one to care for them. Even after the liberation from camps such as Auschwitz, Dachau, and Bergen-Belsen, survivors were again placed in refugee camps and processed, but were without a home or homeland. The British Mandate of 1917 had only allowed a fixed number of Jews to enter Palestine before World War II, and the quota was unacceptable for Zionist nationalists such as David Ben-Gurion to be satisfied. After the war, the British government again declared that only a few families would be allowed into Palestine, due to Arab resistance and protest. The newly formed United Nations had promised the Jews a homeland that would encompass not just what is today the state of Israel but also Trans-Jordan, which is today the Kingdom of Jordan. Again, opposition from the Arab countries made the UN officials reduce the amount of land for a Jewish state to what is Israel today and even that land mass was reduced, with Jordan out as a possible settlement.

In November 1947, fifty years after the declaration of the Zionist cause, The United Nations voted to establish a Jewish homeland in what were the borders of ancient Israel. The Arab countries voted against it, but other nations, including Russia, voted in the affirmative. The British government would leave Palestine and hand it over to Jewish control the next year. On May 14, 1948, meeting in Tel Aviv, the leaders of the Jewish delegation, headed by David Ben-Gurion, declared the birth of the state of Israel. The U.S. President, Harry S. Truman, recognized the new nation fifteen minutes after the declaration, and since then, the US has been the staunchest supporter of Israel, with some rough patches occurring since then. The new nation had to fight for its life the first two years of its existence due to attacks from countries such as Egypt, Jordan, Iraq, and Lebanon.

There has been a tense armistice between Israel and her Arab neighbors since the blistering defeat of a unified Arab army in June 1967, where the Israeli Defense Force captured the city of Jerusalem, the Golan Heights of Syria, and the West Bank of what was Jordan. The nation of Israel has never been out of the public eye and is a major player in technology, defense, agriculture, medicine, and optics. To this day Christians and devout Jews believe that their nation plays a significant role in the prophetic world. Yet, it is primarily a land of unbelief, with most of the Jews living secular lives and only a small number who practice their faith. The widespread unbelief and doubt about God's existence stems from the persecutions that they have had to endure over the centuries, especially the Holocaust.

They would probably argue as to why God allowed them to go through that terrible time of suffering. Yet, they have persevered and thrived in hostile climates and God has preserved them while other nationalities have fallen into the dustbin of history. Genesis 12:1-4 says that God would bless those who bless Israel and curse those who curse it. That edict has not gone out of God's memory or purpose. If you look at how nations have treated the Jews throughout history, many are no longer here due to the violation of this biblical promise. It is an interesting note of history to see how empires and kingdoms have fared due to what they did with the Jews.

During the 1930's, the British government did not allow large numbers of Jews to immigrate to Palestine to escape the growing treachery of Hitler and six million desperate Jews became victims of the gas chambers or unspeakable medical experiments by the Nazis. Winston Churchill, who would become the Prime Minister of England during World war II, had been a staunch advocate of the need for the Jews to resettle their land and establish their own nation, but most of his suggestions were ignored by the respective governments in power, and he was considered insignificant in terms of political importance during the 1930's and powerless to do anything. After the end of the war, the British Empire started to decline as her colonies and dominions became independent or self-governing within twenty years. This started in 1947, when India gained her independence, and concluded in 1967 when Britain's grip on Africa was broken. Today England governs a handful of islands. Her status as a world power has been greatly reduced and depends on US Aid from time to time. Could this situation have been God's judgment on Britain not to harm His people? It is worth examining for the sake of history.

Germany has not fared much better since the end of World War II. Before Adolf Hitler came to power, Jews were living well in the country. After Hitler took power in 1933, he began passing draconian laws which took away German citizenship from the Jews. The laws imposed by Hitler and his cronies in the first years of the Third Reich caused Jewish merchants to close their businesses. Their synagogues were burned or destroyed, and they were soon forced to live in quarantined areas called ghettos, where some starved to death and became a step on the road to the concentration camps. The US and other Allied nations knew about the camps but were unable to do anything. Nazi Germany ruled most of Europe by 1940, and the Allies couldn't put up an attempt to rescue them until they totally destroyed the Nazi war machine in the process. It would not be until the D-Day landings by the Allies in 1944 when the US, Britain, Canada, and other nations stormed the beaches and gained ground, putting an unstoppable force in motion that brought about the fall of the Nazis in May 1945.

The Russians, coming in from the East towards Berlin, discovered the existence of the camps. Allied Supreme Commander Dwight D. Eisenhower visited each of the camps, and the troops under his command immediately began giving the survivors food and aid. He ordered troops to gather every resident of nearby German towns and had them march through the area camps to see what their "Fuhrer" had initiated. After their surrender, Germany was divided into four sections, each governed by a representative Allied power, specifically the USA, Great Britain, France, and Russia. The capital city of Berlin was also divided into four sectors. The Russian government would take their section and transform it into the German Democratic Republic, or East Germany, a nation that would be in existence until the fall of communism in 1989. Berlin would also be divided along East and West lines by a wall that kept the city divided between Communist and free nations also until the wall came down in 1989. Again, we wonder if God was not judging the Germans for their murder of God's people. Even now, there is a rise of Anti-Semitism rising in modern Germany by young people, and the influx of Syrian refugees and radical Islam also is fanning the flames. Muslims in Great Britain and France are openly calling for jihad against Israel. We presently have in the U.S. Congress two representatives who are violent anti-Jew and Christian. They are of the Muslim faith.

There are growing calls for boycotting Israel, with political leftists declaring it to be an "apartheid" state for allegedly not allowing the creation of a Palestinian State with East Jerusalem as the capital. Israel well know that this would bring about war with the governing body of Gaza, Hamas, as well as the wrath of Palestinian Authority Mahmoud Abbas. The increase in Muslim population in the United States is cause for concern, with the fear by most Americans that the Muslim population could outnumber the American citizens within less than fifty years. Should the world still be in its present state at that time, the Scriptures will correctly declare that Israel will be hated by all nations, but for believers in the soon return of the Lord

Jesus Christ and His establishment of an eternal kingdom, that particular concern may not come to pass.

The current chaotic state of the world is clear proof that the Last Days spoken of in Scripture are at hand, if not already in action. With that looming, attention needs to be given to the dry bones of Israel which start the restoration and eventually rebirth of God' chosen people. While Ezekiel 37:1-14 deals with the rise and rebirth of the nation, the remainder of the chapter shows the role of Israel in the future world, united and established as the premier nation on the new Earth.

Ezekiel 37: 15 – 28 reads as follows:

"The word of the LORD came again to me, saying, 'And you, son of man, take for yourself one stick, and write on it, 'For Judah, and for the sons of Israel his companions'; then take another stick and write on it, 'For Joseph, the stick of Ephraim, and all the house of Israel his companions'. Then join them for yourself one to another into one stick, that they become one in your hand'. And when the sons of your people speak to you saying, 'Will you not declare to us what you mean by these? Say to them, 'Thus says the LORD GOD; 'Behold, I will take the stick of Joseph, which is in the hand of Ephraim; and the tribes of Israel his companions, and I will put them with it, with the stick of Judah, and make them one stick, and they will be one in My hand. And the sticks on which you write will be in your hand before their eyes. And say to them, 'Thus Says the LORD GOD; Behold I will take the sons of Israel from among the nations where they have gone, and I will gather them from every side and bring them into their own land, and I will make them one nation in the land on the mountains of Israel, and one king will be king for all of them; and they will no longer be two nations, and they will no longer be divided into two kingdoms.

"And they will no longer defile themselves with their idols, or with their detestable things, or with any of their transgressions, but I will deliver them from all their dwelling places in which they have sinned, and will cleanse them, and they will be my people, and I will be their God. And My servant David will be king over them; and they will all have one shepherd, and they will walk in my ordinances and keep my statutes and observe them. And they shall live on the land that I have gave to Jacob My servant, in which your fathers lived, and they will live on it, they, and their sons, and their sons's sons forever, and David My servant shall be their prince forever. And I will make a covenant of peace with them; it will be an everlasting covenant with them. And I will place them and multiply them and will set My sanctuary in their midst forever. My dwelling place also will be with them, and I will be their GOD, and they will be my people. And the nations

will know that I am the LORD who sanctifies Israel, when My sanctuary is in their midst forever." (NASB).

John MacArthur, the well-known biblical scholar and pastor, writes: *"In verses 15-23, the vision comes to an end, and Ezekiel was given an object lesson that his people observed. This drama of uniting two sticks offered a second illustration that God will not only regather Israelites to their land, but will for the first time since 931 B.C. (The end of Solomon's reign) restore union between Israel and Judah in the Messianic reign (Isaiah 11:1-2; Jeremiah 3:18; Hosea 11:1). God made three promises that summarized His plans for Israel; (1) restoration (v.21); (2) Unification (v.22), and (3) purification (v.23). These promises bring to fulfillment the Abrahamic covenant (Genesis 12), the Davidic covenant (2 Samuel) and the New Covenant (Jeremiah 31) respectively. The new Israel will be governed by the Messiah, Jesus Christ, the descendant of David."*
(1)

William MacDonald writes:

"Verses 15-23: Ezekiel was next commanded to take two sticks, one representing Judah, the other Israel. By holding them end to end, he joined them in one stick. This meant that the two kingdoms would be reunited. One king, the Messiah, would reign over them and they would be saved, cleansed, and restored. In verses 24-28, David (the Lord Jesus) would be the king and the people would obey Him implicitly. God would make an everlasting covenant of peace with them, and the Temple would be set in their midst. This is the future." (2)

The future place in history for Israel will be one of honor, redemption, and peace under the perfect rule of God's Messiah, the Lord Jesus Christ. In the future, there will be tribulation for the nation, but out of it will come the return of Christ to rule and reign as King and Messiah for all time .Let us rejoice at the fact that all things will be made new, and we shall be united, Jew and Gentile in a coming world that will know no suffering or heartache. The Jewish people will be home for all eternity and be the first among nations. That promise from the Word of God is seen by many students and teachers of biblical prophecy as an event that is to occur sooner than a lot of people expect as the days progress.

Chapter 8
The Prophecy against Gog and Magog:
Ezekiel 38 and 39

Ezekiel was not finished with his declaration of Israel's return and vindication. He would give a prophecy against the enemies of Israel who would attempt a plot to destroy them once and for all. This prophecy is to be fulfilled during the period of the nation's restoration at the end of days. The enemy of Israel is a power known as Gog, together with his allies, who will come out of the north to attack the land and be a part of the last battle between God and man, that of Armageddon. Many prophecy scholars and amateur investigators have brought up some varied theories on these nations and where their part is specifically in the end time scenario for Israel. God is not going to stand by and let His people be the victim of a mad dictator, namely the Antichrist and his revived Roman Empire. He will have the final say in the affairs of men, both friend and foe of Israel and more importantly, God Himself.

Some scholars believe that the culprit of Israel's fate is a man or nation referred to in Chapters 38 and 39 as "Gog", the prince of "Rosh", "Meshach" and "Tubal", who comest the land of Israel with her allies Put, Persia, Gomer, and Torgamah with the objective of eradicating the Jewish people once and for all, uniting with the armies of the Beast (Revelation 13). A view put forth by Dr. J. Dwight Pentecost in <u>Things to Come</u> describes these nations and their allies as those who will also align themselves against the Beast of Revelation 13, although the prophetic picture calls for honest debate over the matter.

Notes from related research and speculation also state that Gog is called "the prince of Rosh, Meshach, and Tubal" as indicated above. It is the name of an individual. The land is called Magog, which was a region populated by the descendants of Noah's second son Japheth. Magog's land is what is known today as the region and steppes of the Caucasus Mountains. Rosh, Meshach, and Tubal were called by the ancients Scythians. They roamed the region and were considered barbarians, wandering around the regions of the Black and Caspian Seas. Research has confirmed that Rosh is Russia. Therefore, the prince of Rosh means the king of the Russian Empire. C.I.

Scofield, in his interpretation of these passages, came to the same conclusion when he wrote the notes to his version in the first years of the twentieth century, but wondered how this could be since at that time Russia was considered to be a Christian country. After the fall of the Czar in 1917 and the rise of the Bolshevik government, many prophecy students interpreted this as the rise of communism and its defeat by the hands of the LORD.

To the twentieth century mindset, the Soviet Union was accepted as a permanent fixture in world affairs. When it fell in 1991, this made a lot of prophetic scholars rethink their ideas and hypotheses. After the fall of the Berlin Wall in 1989 and the apparent inability of the Soviets to hold on to their power in Eastern Europe, it was assumed that the Russians would be a weak country. How could this be mighty Gog? It was not long after this episode that a new strong man came on the scene, Vladimir Putin. Through his leadership, he has expanded Russian influence in Europe, the Ukraine, the Crimean Peninsula, and has a hold on Syria, immersed in a bloody civil war, controlling the moves of Syrian President Bashar el-Hafez. Relations between Russia and its rival the United States is strained at best. Putin is a man who has absolute control over the lives of his people and their destiny. He has placed his military in Syria and is aligned with Iran and Turkey at the borders of Israel at this time. At the time of this writing, Israeli Prime Minister Benjamin Netanyahu has flown several times to Moscow to get assurance from Putin that there will be no trouble in the region. Of course, with Iranian soldiers in Syria near the Golan Heights, Israel is understandably nervous. Russia and her allies are now in the Middle East and could strike Israel at any time. It could be possible that this generation could see these events come to pass.

Let us look at the allies of the one known as Gog. The first ally mentioned is the nation of Persia. During the days of the exile, Persia assisted the Jews with the rebuilding of Jerusalem and the establishment of the Second Temple around 483 B.C. Persian rule of the land of Judea was relatively peaceful, except for the plot by the Persian court official Haman to rid the land of the Jews by mass execution. It was the courage of Esther the Queen that foiled this plot and sent Haman to the gallows. Jews lived in Persia for centuries and were a part of the population well into the twentieth century. Iran was ruled by a succession of emperors known as shahs. The most recent Shah was Mohammed Reza Pahlavi (1919-1980), who, during his reign from 1941-1979 had diplomatic relations with Israel and assisted with military strategy for the Israeli Defense Force. The Shah was a staunch ally of the United States and had led Iran in a period of prosperity.

However, there were signs of discontent in the nation that grew exponentially in 1978, leading to the Shah's downfall and exile in January 1979.His rival, Ayatollah Ruhollah Khomeini returned from exile in France and established an Islamic Republic, taking American diplomatic personnel hostage in November 1979, breaking off relations with the US and Israel. The hostages were held for 444 days until the inauguration of Ronald Reagan as President in January 1981. Today Iran is run by the ayatollahs and is a sworn enemy of the Jewish state. Their acts and sponsorship[p of world-wide terrorism is based on a Shia Muslim prophecy that the Islamic Messiah called the Mahdi will not come unless there is violence and upheaval in the world, and the Iranian government is trying to speed that process along. It is a government run by fanatical madmen who wish to see the whole world come under Islamic rule.

Up to January 2021, Iran was under a series of harsh economic sanctions imposed by the United States by order of former President Trump. The cost of essential goods and services is extreme, jobs are scarce, there is constant unrest, protests, and often riots by the citizens in the tens of thousands in almost every city and province in the country, and there are growing calls for not just the ouster of the mullahs, but their deaths. There are continual, yet censored recordings of mass demonstrations calling for the return of the exiled Crown Prince, Reza Pahlavi, and the Christian faith is growing exponentially despite fierce persecution from the Shiite government. If Iran does attack Israel, it will be without the support of a huge majority of Iranian citizens. Perhaps the LORD will spare the nation and destroy the oppressive rule of the clerics and their lackeys. It would be an interesting take on prophetic interpretation.

The second ally mentioned is Ethiopia. The Bible refers to this country nine times, referring to the land below Egypt. It can also mean the land of Cush, which is another name for the area of what is today Arabia. It was probably the eunuch treasurer of Candace the Queen of Ethiopia, who, under the preaching of Phillip the evangelist in Acts 8, brought Christianity to the land and probably spread throughout the African lands through traders and merchants who heard the gospel message in the country. Ethiopia was a nation that was founded upon biblical tales. The constitution of Ethiopia, to this day, says that the union of the Queen of Sheba and Solomon resulted in the birth of Ethiopia's first emperor, Menelik. For centuries afterwards, the land was ruled by a succession of emperors, with the last one being Haile Selassie, who ruled from 1931-1974. Ethiopia had diplomatic relations with Israel, and one of Selassie's title was "Lion of the Tribe of Judah" Haile Selassie was exiled first in 1935 when the forces of fascist Italy, led by Benito Mussolini, invaded the country and set up colonial rule. It ended when World War II came to an end in 1945.

The Emperor was a committed Christian. However, unrest came in the nation, which was led by communist insurgents, who overthrew the government and imprisoned the aged emperor who died in 1975. Ethiopia was declared a republic and broke off diplomatic relations with Israel. The nation went through a severe famine in the 1980's and has never truly recovered. As of now, it does not look like the nation can muster an army to ally themselves with Gog due to its abject poverty. Another suggestion for the land of Cush is, again, that of Arabia and its lands. The land was settled by the descendants of Ishmael, and it is in modern Saudi Arabia where many believe the true Mount Sinai is located, known also as the land of Midian. The inhabitants of this land were and still are nomadic, known as Bedouins. Arabia is also known as the place where the apostle Paul went for three years to learn the doctrines of the faith from the resurrected Christ (Galatians 1:11-17).

It is in the Arabian Peninsula where the Islamic faith was born, led by a merchant named Mohammed. Within a hundred years after his death in 632 A.D., Islam had spread throughout the area of the Middle East, north Africa, and up into what is today Spain. It was halted in France by Charles Martel ("the Hammer") at the battle of Tours in 732. Islamic rule in Jerusalem and the Holy Land was temporarily halted by the Christian Crusaders from 1197 to 1297. The Crusades had been the idea of Pope Urban II in 1195 with the idea of rescuing the Holy Land from the Muslims. The overall campaigns of the Crusades really proved ineffective and was often used as a means of obtaining treasure from invaded lands. Many Muslims and Jews were killed by knights who saw it as their duty to abolish infidel rule in the land of Christ. Muslim rule was also a threat to the Byzantine Empire, which enveloped the land of Asia Minor and the surrounding regions.

The Byzantines ruled from 313 A.D. -1453 A.D. from their capital city Constantinople, which had been established by the Emperor Constantine, who wanted to make the eastern portion of the Roman empire his own. After the fall of the Western Roman Empire in 476 A.D., many Roman citizens fled to Byzantium and settled in an area that had at one time ruled what is now the nation of Turkey, Greece, North Africa, and the Italian Peninsula at its peak in the sixth century A.D. Muslim conquerors nabbed the Middle East and North Africa and slowly started infiltrating more of the empire. Beginning in the 14th century, a group of Muslims known as the Ottoman Turks began aa series of assaults on the Byzantines and slowly gained more ground, eventually conquering them in 1453 and establishing the Ottoman Empire, which included what is today Turkey, Greece, and the Middle East, and would be in power until the early part of the twentieth century.

The end of Ottoman rule came at the conclusion of World War I in 1918. They had allied themselves with Germany and the Austro-Hungarian Empire and were referred to as the Central Powers. The Kaiser of Germany, Wilhelm II, Emperor Karl I of Austria, and Sultan Mehmed VI each lost their thrones and their respective empires. These former imperial possessions were then carved up into sovereign nations in a new post-war Europe and new nations were created in the Middle East, such as Iraq, Syria, Lebanon, and Palestine, which became a British Mandate for the next thirty years. Saudi Arabia, not part of any empire, was formed under the rule of Abdul Aziz bin Saud in 1925, whose family still rules the kingdom today.

Most Arab nations are rich in oil and have used it as a weapon to get other nations to lessen their economic and moral support to Israel. The Saudis have been allies with the United States and have supported excursions into nations like Iraq under Saddam Hussein. As of now, the Saudis and their neighbors have been power players on the world stage and have used their oil wealth to further their Islamic causes. It was a group of nineteen Saudis who flew the planes into the World Trade Center on September 11, 2001. Saudi rule is under Sharia law. Women have few rights and there is punishment for anyone who desecrates Islam. There are also public executions and floggings in the kingdom. Current Crown Prince Mohammed ibn Salman was allegedly in private talks with Israeli officials over what to do about Iran, a mutual enemy. The Prince had also entertained the idea to allow other religions in the kingdom.

Iran has launched missiles into Saudi Arabia and came close in 2019 to severely damaging the capital, Riyadh. The two nations are fighting a proxy war in Yemen with devastating consequences for the citizens of that country such as mass famine and lack of medical and humanitarian assistance. Iran has a goal of invading the kingdom and destroying the Grand Mosque in Mecca, which is a symbol of Sunni Islam, a bitter enemy of the Shiites mainly over an argument over the proper successor of the Prophet that has been going on for over 1300 years. Iran's goal is not just to wipe out Israel, but to be the dominant power in the entirety of the Middle East and to spread terrorism worldwide in order to hasten the return of their Messiah, the Mahdi, who will allegedly put all nations under Islam on the penalty of death for resistance or failure to convert. An estimated 20-30% of all Muslims are defined as radical and will do anything to bring this goal to reality. There is silence on the part of other Muslims who want nothing to do with the fanaticism (at least publicly) on fear of honor killings or Fatwahs.

The next ally of Gog is the land of Put, or modern Libya. This country also has a history of terrorist sponsorship, including attacks against citizens of foreign countries, and threats of destruction of her neighbors, especially Israel. Libya during the days of Roman rule was called Tripolitania and stayed under Roman and Byzantine rule until the time of the Muslim advance from Arabia and the successors of Mohammed. The nation gained a reputation of piracy and slavery as it often intercepted the vessels carrying Crusaders or merchants from Europe and Constantinople. Libyan history with the United States began in around 1807 when pirates from Tripoli abducted American servicemen and held them as hostages or sold them into slavery. U.S. President Thomas Jefferson sent a battalion of Marines to perform a rescue operation and defeat the Tripoli Pirates once and for all. The fight was a victory for the US and the Anthem of the Marine Corps to this day is "to the shores of Tripoli".

In the twentieth century, Libya was annexed by Italy as a colony, which had mixed results. The Libyans fought against the Italians, but Mussolini's armies proved too powerful. It wasn't until the end of World War II that Libya obtained her independence and established a pro-western monarchy which was overthrown in 1969 by a coup under Colonel Moammar Gaddafi, who quickly established a dictatorship and began a series of terrorist attacks against Israel and her allies. The 1972 kidnapping and killing of Israeli athletes at the Olympic Games in Munich, West Germany was the work of the Libyans. In the 1980's under the Reagan Administration, there were alleged "death squads" sent out by Gaddafi to kill the President without success. In 1985 the Libyan government took responsibility for the bombing of a West German nightclub where several

U.S. soldiers were killed. President Reagan had enough of it and in April 1986 ordered a systematic bombing of Tripoli and the Libyan coast as retaliation for the killings.

After that, the world heard no more of Gaddafi's actions and the country went into self-imposed isolation. When the terrorists flew the planes into the World Trade Center on September 11, 2001, Colonel Gaddafi quickly proclaimed that he had nothing to do with it, diverting attention away from him. Libya stayed quiet until the "Arab Spring" of 2011, where the Obama Administration gave its approval to the overthrow of dictators on the North African coast, including Gaddafi, who was shot to death by a mob. The "Arab Spring" was chaotic, and Libya fell into a state of anarchy, with no clear leader and it became a haven for ISIS troops. As of now, Libya is not able or willing to enter into any kind of agreement with the nations who will make up the Northern Confederacy. It is a nation in trouble with no one at the helm, but as of late 2021, reports are that one of the sons of the former dictator Gaddafi is ready to assume power if elected the country's President.

Another ally of Gog is the land of Gomer, specifically what is now the nation of Germany. The Talmud, the Jewish book of traditions, laws, and comments on Scripture state that the land of Gomer was populated by tribes known as the Germania. The barbarians who constantly fought with the Roman Empire were from the land of Germania. As Rome slowly lost her grip on Europe, they recruited Germans as soldiers to keep the boundaries of the empire safe. During the post-Roman world, the Germania settled into varied states and were not part of any particular kingdom until the 9th century under the Emperor Charlemagne, who on Christmas Day 800, had himself crowned by the Pope to establish the Holy Roman Empire, which lasted until 1814.

The German states were part of this loosely knit "empire" which never really exerted much power, although there were efforts by respective emperors to wield influence over Rome and other monarchies in Europe, but as far as history goes, it was neither holy, Roman, or an empire, but a loosely organized quagmire of peoples and states, including the Germans. A notable episode in the history of the Empire was that Emperor Charles V presided over the trial of reformer Martin Luther at the Diet of Worms in 1521. Luther, an Augustinian monk, had begun to read the Bible and rediscovered the doctrine of justification by faith in Christ alone for salvation. He boldly proclaimed that neither the popes nor the rituals of Catholicism were needed to gain access to heaven. The church hierarchy soon put Luther on trial where he was told to recant his teachings and beliefs. Luther refused, was put away in a castle for his safety, and began to write and teach upon the exclusivity of Jesus Christ as Savior. He began the Protestant Reformation, and soon word of Luther's sermons and teaching spread throughout the German states. Lutheranism is still considered part of the German culture but has little influence now.

Germany as a nation did not unite until 1871, when the German Empire was formed with Wilhelm I as Kaiser, German for "Caesar", and the work of statesman Otto Von Bismarck. He saw the rise of Wilhelm II in 1888, who strengthened the Empire and made it a powerful voice in European affairs. The Kaiser showed off the strength of Imperial Germany, especially its military. Through a series of accusations and vows of defense among the empires of Europe, World War I broke out, lasting from 1914-1918, with Germany at the head of what was known as the Central Powers, along with Austria-Hungary and the Turks. The war stagnated until the arrival of US troops in 1917. They, along with the Allied powers of Great Britain and France, brought an end to the war as well as the German Empire in November 1918.

Germany was blamed for the war and ordered to pay the war debt. Observers and diplomats at the Versailles Conference in 1919 warned that this excessive burden on the Germans would only start the fire for a new war within twenty years. The Kaiser abdicated and went into exile in Holland where he died in 1941. Germany was broke, and destitute, with a weak government at its center. In 1923 a radical socialist by the name of Adolf Hitler began his rise to power as the head of the National Socialist Party, or Nazis. He gained a following, promising the German people that they were the "master race", destined for greatness and prosperity if they would but follow him. In 1933 Hitler became chancellor of Germany and put the nation under total Nazi control, targeting the Jews for persecution and later, execution. His actions brought about World War II, which lasted from 1939-1945. Hitler and his evil regime were brought down by the combined forces of the US and Great Britain. Post-war relationships were begun by Konrad Adenauer (1876-1967), former chancellor of West Germany, with Israel in the early 1950's, and there is still a nominal diplomatic relationship today, but as stated earlier, there is a growing hatred of Jews not just in Germany, but all over Europe. Sometime in the future, the Germans may gladly join Gog in its mission to destroy the nation of Israel.

The next ally of Gog to receive notice is that of Tog Armah. This nation is now known today as Turkey, Armenia, and the Asiatic areas. We will concentrate on Turkey, which was formerly the seat of power in the Ottoman Empire, which ruled the regions of Asia Minor and the Middle East from 1453-1918. After the disposal of the Ottoman Sultan Mehmed VI, the nation looked to a new leader named Kamal Ataturk, who established the country as a secular state, Muslim but not with a mind to expand its influence anywhere. Ataturk led Turkey and modernized it until his death in 1938. The country stayed neutral in World War II despite Allied attempts to bring the nation into the war. After the war, Turkey joined the newly formed agency NATO (North Atlantic Treaty Organization) to safeguard itself against Soviet expansion, which was a real threat, especially in Europe. Turkey was the first Muslim majority state to recognize the state of Israel in 1949, one year after its declaration as a nation. Israel and Turkey have had good relations and did joint military exercises over the years, until the rise of Turkish President Tyapp Erdogan, who assumed power in 2014, and was given executive powers to govern by a narrow vote in 2017. Up to that time, the presidential office had been largely ceremonial. Erdogan has threatened in the past to break off diplomatic ties with Israel if the US recognized Jerusalem as its capital.

No further action has been taken to date, except that now Turkey is allied with Russia and Iran and is seen as a potential threat to the stability of the region. At of the time of this writing, Russia and Iran were in Syria. Turkey is saber-rattling with its support of what is going on in the region. Due to the rise in Muslim immigrants in key European countries, many nations who had been friendly with Israel have started to wobble diplomatically. The United Nations keeps on singling out Israel, with some nations calling for sanctions, boycotts, protests, and ending diplomatic relations with countries again, for its alleged treatment of the Palestinians. However, the Palestinians are harboring terrorist groups like Hamas in the Gaza Strip and Hezbollah in Lebanon and are supported by Iran. The world is sitting on a powder keg and the stage is set for war. How will this come out and what could be the scenarios?

We know from prophetic Scriptures that God has decreed a massive war in the region. There are several interpretations of how this war will originate, engage, and end. First, there are those who say that we will be witnesses to it just before the Rapture of the church and events noted in Psalm 83, which tell of a group of nations coming together to destroy Israel, but God will give Israel the victory and expand its land. This could be a real possibility. Nothing needs to occur for the powder keg to explode internationally. Second, there is the possibility of the war taking place after the Rapture of the church. Here is a possible scene. When the Christians are gone, the United States could be taken over by Socialists who despise Israel and want nothing to do with her, joining in support of the war. The US could become a weaker influence in world affairs, too, because a sizeable portion of the population will be gone and there will be no voice for the Jews. All the nations will be aligned against Israel and will champion the Northern Confederacy. When these forces are destroyed by God, the world and Israel will know it was a sovereign act of the LORD. Israel will seek peace with her defeated neighbors, and a treaty will be put forth, signed by the World Leader (the Antichrist) and the nation for seven years of peace, which will soon be short lived.

Some prophecy scholars see the Gog-Magog War as a symbol for the last battle between God and Satan, with the future of Israel in the balance. Some believe it refers to the Battle of Armageddon, where the forces of the Beast and his allies will wage war against Israel and attempt to destroy the Jews once and for all. This is the time when Israel will call for her Messiah. He comes in the form of the Lord Jesus Christ to destroy the armies of the Beast and send him and the False Prophet into the Lake of Fire.

This war is short-lived. God will use earthquakes, pestilence, a bloody battle between the armies, flooding rain, hailstones, and fire and brimstone to destroy these foes of Him and his people. He will use absolute disaster to fall upon them. The result is a sea of dead bodies that will take seven months to bury, and many of the bodies will end up being consumed by scavenger birds. The weapons of war will burn for seven years, and Israel's restoration will be complete and their Messiah, King Jesus will be with the victor.

Chapter 9
Jesus' Declaration of the Last Days: The Prologue

The events recorded in Scripture are written to show that what we refer to as history is not a quagmire of unrelated events and circumstances that were brought about by a whim or sudden action that began a chain of experiences and quickly calculated solutions that brought some semblance of order for a brief time. If anything, what has been just described is a belief or observation grounded on the Darwinian idea of random selection and what is referred to by some as "the survival of the fittest", which applies to animal and human life in the evolutionary drama.

This worldly and dark method of thought stands in sharp contrast to the Bible, which presents history as planned times of development, thinking, nationalism, legal structure, and sense of purpose and meaning that are in line with the plans and ideas of the Sovereign God of the Universe, Whom Scripture affirms as the Almighty Creator, Moral Lawgiver, Absolute Standard of Righteousness, Goodness, and Salvation, who will bring all things to an appropriate ending with Him receiving all glory and honor from His redeemed people for having all events under His control and to bring all evil acts, thoughts, and people to face certain, inescapable, final judgment and given due and just punishment lasting for eternity.

The true center of all history and civilization is the Lord Jesus Christ, noted by all objective historians and scholars as the most influential person who ever lived. Aside from the references found in the Scriptures, many noted individuals have stated opinions, observations, and beliefs about Him. He and His words have been loved, adored, studied, honored, admired, imitated, desecrated, mocked, and hated, but there is yet anyone, redeemed or reprobate, who has ever been neutral about Him. People throughout the ages since He lived on this earth have given their lives to Him or have determined to eliminate any mention of His name, and too often these same infidels die screaming for His mercy as their lives slipped into a horrendous eternity. To read the final words of unbelievers such as the French philosopher Voltaire and the author of "The Age of Reason" by the

Revolutionary War hero Thomas Paine are tragic and frightening and should serve as a sobering call for repentance.

While there is an abundance of evidence outside the Scriptures which verify the existence and message of Jesus Christ in Roman history and Jewish works such as Josephus, the Babylonian Talmud, the Mishnah and other sources that have been presented earlier, it is the Scriptures themselves which present Jesus Christ in all His glory and honor, and tell of His mission, purpose and teaching. After His ascension, His apostles declared that He would return to rule and reign over the earth and conquer all evil for good. The Scriptures describe the Second Coming of Christ as "The Day of the LORD" (1 Thessalonians 5:2), the Day of the Lord Jesus (1 Corinthians 5:5), "that Day" (2 Thessalonians 1:10), and the apostle John wrote of it in his Gospel (John 12:48).

The Bible's teachings are clear as to the purpose of Christ's Second Coming. It will be a total fulfillment of His Word (John 14:3), it will be the promised time of the resurrection of the dead in Christ (1 Thessalonians 4:13-18), referred to as "the Blessed Hope", or "the Rapture". His arrival will mean the destruction of death (1 Corinthians 15:25, 26), the gathering of His elect (Matthew 24:31) and the judgment of the world (Matthew 25:32-46). It will be the time where all believers in Christ will be glorified, given new, sinless, ageless, perfect bodies (Colossians 3:4), and they will be given their rewards for serving and living for Him (Matthew 16:27).

His coming is near. However, we do not know the hour or the day (Matthew 24: 27, 36). A major sign that His return is certain is when the Gospel is proclaimed around the world (Matthew 24:14). He will return after the final stand of the Antichrist against the many repentant souls who have turned to Him for salvation during the time of the Great Tribulation (2 Thessalonians 2:2, 3). Paul speaks of the Lord's return at the sound of the last trumpet (1 Corinthians 15:51, 52). The Lord Jesus also said that His arrival would be as unexpected as the flood that wiped out the wicked generation of Noah (Matthew 24:37-47).

Many books, sermons, and teachings concerning the signs of the end times Jesus spoke of have listed the current events of their respective situation as it pertains to world and national affairs, and soon after their work is published or presented, the material that had been used as evidence suddenly needs to be revised or updated. An example would be prophetic interpretations of how the former Soviet Union would spread their evil of communism, only to be stopped by the LORD at the Battle of Gog and Magog, which was examined earlier. Many prophetic books were written at the height of the "Cold War" (1945-1991), when nearly everyone assumed that Russia and its neighbors would be under the rule of Marx and Lenin for all time.

When former Soviet President Michael Gorbachev dissolved the USSR in 1991 and allowed all the countries under its grip to go free, many prophecy scholars were turned on their heads and had to rethink the pattern on how events would occur because of this monumental change in international relations. Few diplomats or political scientists were paying much attention to the growing threat of radical Islamic thought in areas of the Middle East, save for the rhetoric and hatred of the West by the nation of Iran under the control of the ayatollahs and their lackeys. However, after the terrorist attacks on September 11, 2001, in New York, Washington, and Pennsylvania, some prophecy experts started to read and examine the writings found in the Koran concerning the end of days, and how radicals were attempting to usher in the arrival on Earth of the "Twelfth Imam", or "Mahdi", who would, with his associate Prophet Jesus, establish Islam around the world and eliminate all infidels who will not convert. Islam now is more in favor with the West and the elites, and criticism of it is at the point of total silence.

In light of the explosion of Islamic terrorism over the past two decades since 9/11, some Bible teachers and political researchers have started looking at the characteristics of the Muslim Mahdi, and most have concluded that this figure might be the biblical Antichrist spoken of in passages such as 2 Thessalonians, Daniel 11, and Revelation 13. It should be stated that there are honest disagreements between brethren concerning this interpretation, and no one should break fellowship or start frictions over this topic. Many prophetic experts maintain that the "Beast" will arise out of a revived Roman Empire that will replace the economically and socially crumbling European Union, a conglomerate of nationalities that many saw as a sure fulfillment of prophecy.

The European Union has really never been a stable governing force in light of the demands it made upon member nations in areas of energy production and consumption, trade, the taxes, and the belief by some that the EU was the end of national sovereignty for member nations as well as the end of their respective histories. In 2016, the United Kingdom presented a referendum on whether to remain in the EU or re-establish their individual national identity and the freedom to do business with other countries without the approval of the European Parliament. It was known as "Brexit" and was championed by a member of the EU who was a British subject named Nigel Farage. His campaign in favor of Britain exiting the EU met with a 52% approval by the nation but was not finalized until 2020 with the landslide election of a new Conservative government headed by the former mayor of London Boris Johnson, who became Prime Minister.

Other nations in the EU such as Greece, Italy, and possibly France are also making it known to the officials in Brussels that they may want out as well. If this does happen the EU will collapse, making it more than likely for a new form of government that would be less likely to tolerate such national dissent, and that would be the probable scene when the Antichrist comes to power amidst the international chaos that will be happening after the events of the Rapture.

At the time of this writing, world attention is being paid towards China, described in the Bible as one of the "Kings of the East" (Revelation 16:12). Reports from anonymous sources and world health officials have found that the Communist nation had released a viral component known as COVID-19 into the city of Wuhan and infected almost all of the population, who were forcibly quarantined and in many cases left to fend for themselves, with numerous deaths being covered up by the government. The "coronavirus" has spread from China throughout the world and has bought nations and their economies to a standstill. The United States economic powerhouse has been hit hard, and there have been several thousand deaths which prompted the respective governing bodies to shut down "non-essential" public areas and places where people gather as a precaution against its spread, causing businesses to close and a rise in U.S. unemployment to 20% or more. At the time of this writing (2021) the economy of the U.S. is still suffering not only due to the confusing and dictatorial procures and policies from the Biden Administration concerning the COVID situation, but energy production has been decimated by executive orders and inept decisions from bureaucrats who know nothing of private sector business procedures, basic capitalism, or the free market.

Some governors did put in place what some have called draconian measures on their states in the name of "public safety" and have arrested violators, and pastors in particular, for having worship services without permission or approval. Many citizens have protested what they see and declare as violations of civil liberties and the U.S. Constitution. Others have perceived this incident as a planned attack upon the current U.S. administration as retaliation by powerful individuals known as the "deep state". They are punishing America for correcting international trade violations, the restriction on illegal immigration, economic growth and nationalism in the face of growing acceptance of a globalist society, and the defense of religious and civil freedoms, Christianity, among other issues. There have been worldwide protests against government mandates and vaccinations, and political fortunes have started to swing back to conservativism in state and local elections, but it might be a case of too little, too late.

The embrace of the call for "public safety" at the sacrifice of individual liberty is gaining a favorable momentum, and another "pandemic", or other international crisis will more than likely see this become more of a reality than some expect or approve. More and more, there is an increasing censorship of social media posts, public forums, free speech on college campuses, a call to boycott or limit conservative or Judeo-Christian alternatives to secularist thought or action, and the loss of objective reporting of news and information in order to promote agendas that are in direct conflict with the standards upon which our nation was built. It would be irresponsible to say that these times are a mere flow of history that will divert into something more positive and beneficial to new generations in the name of "tolerance", "brotherhood", "diversity", or "oneness", all catch words for "we are our own masters and will run things the way we see fit", a sure sign of the accuracy of the Scriptures in the light of describing human nature (Romans 1:18-32; 3:10-18; Proverbs 10:19; 14:21; 24:9; James 4:17; 1 John 1:8; 3:4; 5:17).

Chapter 10

Jesus' Declaration of the Last Days: The Coming Events

An entire book on the present days in light of biblical prophecy could be written with more than sufficient evidence to affirm these times, but it is better to specifically list the signs of the last days in light of the words of the Lord Jesus in Matthew 24, Mark 13, and Luke 21. Each account will be examined in the light of God's Word, which is final and true (2 Timothy 3:16; Hebrews 4:12; John 17:17). The scene for the respective discourses occurs during the final week of Jesus' public ministry which began after His entry into Jerusalem (Matthew 21:1-11; Mark 11:1-11; Luke 19:28-40; John 12: 12-19). As He enters on a colt, fulfilling the prophecy of Zechariah 9:9, the Pharisees, who have been trying to any excuse to try and be rid of Him since the start of His ministry, tell Him to rebuke the cheering crowds that have greeted Him on His arrival. He responds that nature itself would cheer Him if people were to be silenced (Luke 19: 40). He knows that these cries of praise will be replaced by calls for His death in a matter of days, such is the fickleness of people as well as the influence of Satan to turn them away from the very One who came to call His lost sheep to return to Him (Matthew 10: 6).

The compassion and care He had for His people as a mother hen would have for her brood is presented as a lament and prediction of destruction over Jerusalem. He grieved over the fact that most of the nation of Judea rejected Him as the Promised Messiah, and now would face impending judgment from God for their deliberate spiritual blindness. He brought His disciples to the Mount of Olives just outside the city gates and told them that the Temple, so revered by the Jewish people and the center of worship, would be torn down to the point where there would be nothing left of it but ruins (Matthew 24:2: Mark 13:2; Luke 21:5-6). This was a shock to the disciple's entire concept of who they were as a people and nation. Their idea of the new Messianic age, with Jesus as the conqueror over the forces of Caesar and the rule of Israel over the known world would be shattered by what the Lord was fixing to tell them. Asking Him when these events would take place, He laid out for them a grim future for civilization that would get progressively worse. What is defined as "the last days" in the study of biblical prophecy shows us that we are not in charge of this world's destiny. We will not destroy God's creations in and of our own strength and finite wisdom, nor will this universe simply of its own accord cease to exist (2 Peter 3:10; Revelation 21:1-7).

Jesus described the progression of civilization, not to greatness, but to certain judgment for its growing wickedness and hatred towards God and His people, and the terrifying conclusion. Matthew 24 and 25, Mark 13, and Luke 21 all give the description of what will happen in future times. Of the three descriptions, Matthew writes the most detailed record of what our LORD said would happen, first, as a warning to his fellow Jews of an impending judgment for their refusal to see Jesus as the prophesied Messiah and His mission of redemption for their sakes as well as the world around them. The second reason for this upcoming national disaster was to show them that the old ways of worship and sacrifice were no longer needed or would be accepted by God as a means of atonement because Jesus' death on the cross was the final atonement that would ever be needed. The pure life and blood of Christ that was shed would cleanse men from their sins and bring them out of eternal death into life everlasting, far better than what an animal sacrifice could provide (Isaiah 53:4; John 15:13, 18:14, 2 Corinthians 8:9; Galatians 1:4; Ephesians 5:2; Titus 2:14; Hebrews 9:26; 1 Peter 3:18; 1 John 3:16; Revelation 1:5).

Jesus states in Matthew 24:1-7, that there would be the rise of false teachers. Wars, famines, and earthquakes. These would be signs that would verify His words, but also a signal to those who are spiritually alert that His arrival would not be far off. The Scriptures tell us of the coming wolves that would try and tear the flock of Christ apart (Matthew 5:19, 15:9, 14, 23:16, 24:23; Luke 6:39, 11:52, 17:23; Acts 15:24; 2 Corinthians 11:4, 13; Galatians 1:9; 5:8; Philippians 1:15; 1 Timothy 4:3; Titus 1:11; 2 Peter 2:1-2; 2 John 10; Revelation 2:2). There would also be those who would claim to be prophets, but were charlatans and deceivers (Matthew 7:15, 22: 24;11, 24; Mark 13:22; Luke 6:26, 21:8; Acts 13:6; 2 Corinthians 11:13; 2 Peter 2;1, and 1 John 4:1).

Wars were to be fought in every century following Jesus' times. Nations would arise from the ashes of empires and would unleash times of bloodshed and slaughter in order to crush their enemies, conquer other nations and kingdoms, for vengeance, and the need for security and stability free from threats by other peoples. Some wars have been just, and others a waste of men and material in the name of self-centered power. Wars had been a part of Israel's ancient history with leaders such as David, the beloved warrior king of the past. However, it was the twentieth century that witnessed the greatest amount of warfare and destruction with many nations coming under brutal dictatorships that would not experience freedom for decades. The century began with moods of optimism and the belief that man was able to usher in a new era of peace and prosperity, with contemporary theologians teaching that this coming century may be the period of time where the millennial reign of Christ would become a possibility.

The advances in technology and industrial development and the perceived stability and might of the empires of Russia, under Czar Nicholas II, Germany with Kaiser Wilhelm II, the British Empire under the reigns of Edward VII and his successor George V, along with the emerging world power of the United States, seemed to be the makings of what would be a wondrous time to live and experience. The utopian ideals of what was known as the "Gilded Age" were soon shattered beginning in 1912 with the loss of the "unsinkable" RMS Titanic, a floating palace of varied luxuries and the beauty of exquisite design, planning for years of comfortable transatlantic travel. One of the designers, after the ship was completed and set to go on its maiden voyage on April 10, made an arrogant statement that "God Himself couldn't sink this ship." By April 14 at 2:20 A.M. in the freezing Atlantic, the Titanic was at the bottom of the ocean with the loss of over 1,500 lives from all classes of passengers. Most of the survivors froze to death. 715 people from varied walks of life survived their lives forever changed by the horror they witnessed. The ship was not found until 1986 by Dr. Robert Ballard and his Woods Hole Maritime Expedition based in Massachusetts. Since then, much of the luggage, silverware, dishes, flatware, and various items have been brought up and are now on exhibit at museums worldwide. Since then, the ship has rapidly deteriorated and will be gone in another fifty years or sooner. The tragedy brought about new safety procedures and equipment, improved navigation systems and communications, and thorough inspections of all structures before and after a voyage. Movies and documentaries have been made over the years about the disaster, and every conclusion is that it could have been avoided. Human pride in the latest technology brought about a senseless tragedy.

Two years later, in July of 1914, the killing of the heir to the throne of the Austria-Hungarian Empire brought about a chain reaction of nations coming to the defense of allied nations and people that started World War I, resulting in the deaths of over 40,000,000 by the end in 1918, and the collapse of the empires of Germany, Russia, Austria, and the Turkish Ottomans. The Imperial family of Russia lost their lives and others went into exile and put Europe into a time of confusion, anarchy, hunger, and planting the seeds for another war as well as the rise of brutal dictators such as Hitler, Mussolini, and Franco. The chaos in Russia that had been brought about by the Communists under Vladimir Lenin brought about a civil war that lasted from 1917-1921, ending in over 10,000,000 deaths and the total grip of Communism over the land for the next 74 years until its dissolvement in 1991 by the last Communist leader, Michael Gorbachev.

The bloodshed of the next major conflict, World War II, started by the Nazis in a quest for world domination and aided by Italy and Japan, resulted in over 60,000,000 deaths of soldiers and civilians alike between 1939-1945. That generation of veterans are dying at the estimated rate of 1,500 per day being in their late 90's on average. Within 20 years or less, all the men and women who fought in that war will be gone, and we will have only written records, museums, and film by which they will be remembered. Five short years after the end of World War II, the Communists of North Korea invaded the South in June 1950 in order to conquer it and put it under the iron fist of Kim-Il- Sung, the leader of the North. This resulted in a war for the freedom of South Korea that lasted until 1953 with an armistice between the two nations that is still in existence today, yet technically it has not ended the war itself. The American forces sent to assist the South Koreans experienced over 45,000 known casualties, and only recently has North Korea sent home the remains of American personnel to be interred in national cemeteries. This was made possible through the efforts and threats of international sanctions on the hermit country by the administration of President Donald Trump in 2018.

The conflict in Vietnam (1959-1975) was a quagmire of political indecisions, restricted rules of engagement, brutal retaliation by the communist Vietcong, demonstrations back in the U.S., and the shameful treatment of the soldiers coming home from the war itself. Under the Nixon administration, the strategy of continual air strikes on the Northern Vietnamese capital of Hanoi and the destruction of key installations by American and South Vietnamese troops ended with a peace treaty signed by both sides in 1973 in Paris. We won, but politicians in Washington did not keep the promises of supplying the South Vietnamese government with armaments but without American troop involvement and brought about through their refusal to honor the treaty the fall of South Vietnam in April

1975 and the brutal takeover by the Communists. The verbal debates about the merits of fighting there and the treatment of Vietnam veterans still go on today, almost fifty years after the end of the conflict.

We also got involved in Middle Eastern affairs in August of 1990, when Iraqi President Saddam Hussein's troops invade neighboring Kuwait and annexed it. A coalition of international troops led by U.S. President George H.W. Bush (1924-2018) and British Prime Minister Margaret Thatcher (1925-2017) and other NATO and Arab allies under the supreme command of U.S. General Norman Schwarzkopf. The conflict itself was over in less than 100 hours and brought about a wave of patriotic fervor in the U.S. and a new affection for the armed services that had not been around for decades.

This first Gulf War ended with 200 casualties, who were honored by the Bush Administration and the Allied forces. Ten years later, on September 11, 2001, two airplanes hit the World Trade Center in New York City, causing the buildings to burn and suddenly collapse, killing over 3,000 people and triggering the present "War on Terror" that has been a part of the administrations of three Presidents, George W. Bush (2001-2009), Barack Obama (2009-2017), and Donald Trump (2017-2021). We sent troops to Afghanistan in October 2001 with the objective of capturing the mastermind of the attack, Osama Bin Laden, presumably hiding in a cave protected by the Jihadist Taliban armies who were bent on conquering the nation for sharia Islam and the killing of "infidels" who did not agree with their radical ideology. In August of 2021 the Biden Administration pulled our forces of Afghanistan as the Taliban were rapidly gaining control of the country. In the process we left behind our own countrymen, Afghani aides who would certainly be killed, and over $85 billion dollars of military equipment that are now in the enemy's hands and who have imposed sharia law over the country with its bloody consequences. This withdrawal was a debacle and a stain on our reputation as a country who would look out for the welfare of its allies. Brexit advocate Nigel Farage has rightly said that because of this inexcusable military and diplomatic fiasco, our allies will never trust us again.

The Lord Jesus also warned about the coming of famine worldwide. This tragedy was all too often a part of life in the ancient world, where the population either thrived or diminished due to the outcome of the crops that were harvested. The Roman Empire itself experienced a famine under the reign of Claudius Caesar (Acts 11:28) which prompted the churches to gather food and money to those who were hardest hit by the famine. The apostle Paul would help in many instances and send fellow believers to render assistance where most needed. Famine was also a part of the Old Testament world, often as an instrument of judgment for either the wickedness of the nation or as a strategic method of defeating an enemy nation. The days of the prophets Elijah and Elisha witnessed such occurrences.

Today famine poses to be a worldwide disaster. As of 2020 -2021, swarms of locusts have covered a large portion of equatorial Africa, devouring all crops and plants in their path and leaving nothing to gather or harvest for the nations there. This swarm was headed for the regions of southern Asia and China but has not been reported for several months due to the coronavirus (COVID-19) that spread worldwide from China to all continents. Due to the spread of the virus, which has killed an estimated 3,000,000 people around the globe, meat processing plants and food services have been hit economically, bringing about widespread unemployment and shortages in grocery stores here in America.

Numerous shelves are bare and transporting produce is risky due to truckers catching the virus and infecting their cargoes. Fields full of vegetables are essentially rotting or are given away by farmers so as not to prevent waste. The same goes for poultry, pork, dairy products, and other foods. It is highly probable that unless the nation attempts to get back to work, we will see starvation occur in what was a land of plenty. The last century has been a continual scene of famines caused by wars, deliberate plans of hostile governments, natural disasters, and poor harvests due to weather or other factors. This list gives a tragic numerical account of the ravages of hunger:

China, from 1907 to 1911, saw 25,000,000 dead from starvation. This beleaguered nation would experience waves of famines in 1936 (5,000,000 dead); World War II (3,000,000), and the rule of Mao Zedong and the Communists with over 15,000,000 to 40,000,000 dying of hunger between 1959-1961. Vietnam after World War II experienced a famine that took the lives of anywhere from 400,000 to 2,000,000. Famines in the country of Lebanon cost the lives of 200,000 between 1914 and 1918. Persia suffered from extreme famine in 1917 and 1918 with 8,000,000 to 16,000,000 dying of hunger. The west African nation of Morocco, over an eight -year period (1940-1948) suffered from a lack of food and lost nearly 200,000 lives, respectively.

Ever since the Russian Revolution of 1917 that toppled the Romanov dynasty, the nation has experienced waves of mass hunger and death by the hands of their former Communist masters. The Russian Civil War of 1917-1921 brought about a total of 5,000,000 deaths from a lack of food. The murderous leader Joseph Stalin used a man-made famine in 1932-1933 to bring the rebellious Ukraine region under total Soviet control by seizing property and denying farmers access to their lands to plant crops. The result was anywhere from 7,000,000 to 10,000,000 deaths from this barbaric method of national submission. In World War II, the Nazi juggernaut rolled into the outskirts of the coastal city of Leningrad (formerly St. Petersburg), surrounded the city and stopped all supplies from entering it, resulting in over 1,000,000 citizens dead from mass starvation for over a year before the Soviet army broke through in late 1942 and supplied Leningrad once again with food and other necessities.

Communist insurgency brought down the African nation of Ethiopia and its long ruling Emperor Haile Selassie in 1974, resulting in a decade long famine that caught world attention and a call for aid. All food and supplies were confiscated by the government upon arrival in the aftermath of this attention and the nation would not see any relief until the late 1980's with the fall of the Communist regime and the establishment of an elected republic friendly to Christians and the allowance of farmers and workers to re-establish the shattered economy. The lack of food was also a concern for the nation of the Congo, a former Belgian colony in the center of Africa. Internal warfare and tribal conflicts have caused over 3,000,000 -4,000,000 Congolese to die of starvation. Sub-Saharan Africa, specifically nations hostile to Christianity such as the Sudan have used starvation tactics to rid themselves of all citizens who have objected to Islamic rule. Sanctions towards the Islamic Republic of Iran resulted in shortages of necessities such as food imports and have brought about frequent demonstrations and calls for the death of the Ayatollahs running the country, although the mainstream media tends not to report those stories out of fear or support for Islam and its use of terror to silence critics.

Another sign Jesus gave to signal His return would be the rise and spread of varied diseases and plagues that would end up killing millions over the centuries. Diseases that we thought to be extinct or minimal in scope have returned as a result of social views and the laxation of basic hygiene in respective nations. Diseases such as bubonic plague and leprosy, long thought to have been extinct, have now crept into cities where there is an abundance of homeless individuals who have not been tested for any traces of contamination or obvious illnesses. They live in squalor and filth, often defecating and urinating openly in the streets and public areas, and are taking drugs, with needles found on pavements and in areas where there are large areas of pedestrian traffic. Garbage has piled up in some areas and remain uncollected, and felons are rarely apprehended by law enforcement for fear of retaliation by homeless groups. This is the scene in cities such as Los Angeles and San Francisco, along with other cities that protect illegals and have resisted federal intervention. This had started to change due to measures taken by the Trump Administration's Department of Justice and active apprehensions by border agents but has been dismantled and ignored by the present-day administration and its sycophants in the media and upper echelons of power.

There has been a steady increase in childhood diseases such as mumps, rubella, whooping cough, and chicken pox due to parental resistance to vaccinations, originated and promoted mostly by activist celebrities and those who are suspicious of medical procedures in general. Many physicians have advised that babies and toddlers due for vaccinations such as MMR be done over a period of months, not all at once as has been done in the past and to encourage parents to do objective research on these issues and avoid social media rants and conspiracies. However, in the light of COVID-19, there are companies and foundations that are calling for all people worldwide to partake of a vaccine that will also be used through implanted chips to track movements and could be a form of "mark" written about in the book of Revelation, Chapter 13 specifically. Viruses and diseases among livestock and wild animals are also expanding rapidly. State animal mortality reports and data gathered from websites dealing in related studies since 2011 have shown that millions of fish, thousands of cattle, turkeys, wild birds, deer, buffalo, game animals and domesticated have died due to bacterial infections, natural disasters, lack of oxygen in the waters, pollution, nuclear accidents (such as the 2011 Japan reactor disaster), and dead spots in the oceans where no life is found.

As frightening as these situations are, more is to come according to the Lord Jesus. These continuing troubles will come in the form of increasing earthquakes, growing persecution of the church, and the rise of lawlessness and anarchy, godless behavior and immoral practices, the approval by society of lifestyles and sexual deviancies that target the helpless and vulnerable, and the increasing depravity of humanity in general (Matthew

101

24:27; 27:51, 28:2; Mark 13:8; Luke 21:11; Acts 16:26; Jeremiah 1:19, 15:20; Daniel 7:21, 25; 11;33; Matthew 5:11; 10:17, 23: 13:21; 20:23; 23:34; 24:9; Mark 4:17; 10:30, 39; Luke 6:22; 11:49; 12;11; 21:12; John 9:22; 15:20; 16:2; 21:18; Acts 21:11; Romans 1:18-32; 3:10-18;Galatians 3:4; 1 Thessalonians 3:4; 2Timothy 3:12; Hebrews 10:32; 1 Peter 3:14; 4:12; 3 John 10; Revelation 2:10; 11:17; 13:15).Little wonder that John, at the end of his vision of the Revelation, wrote, "Even so, come Lord Jesus." (Revelation 22:20) and we, who look forward to His coming, are ready to go home and be with Him always? (John 14:1-3; 1 Corinthians 15:51-58; 1 Thessalonians 4:13-18; Revelation 3:10). The Lord concludes with His declaration of what prophecy scholars have called the coming "Great Tribulation" (24:15-28), initiating a period where the Jews will have to flee from the wrath of the Antichrist, who will place a figure of himself inside the Holy of Holies in the rebuilt Temple in Jerusalem and declare himself God. He will begin a worldwide violent persecution of the Jewish people and all who do not take his mark or bow to him. Many will be killed, but a remnant will be protected by the hand of God and hidden from the wrath of this individual known as "the Beast". These will be delivered by the coming of Jesus Christ, who is their Messiah, destroying the works of darkness and to establish His eternal rule on a new earth (Revelation 19:11-21).

In Israel today, there are reports of an estimated 50,000 Messianic Jews, and those Jews who consider themselves secular are now allegedly expressing an interest in spiritual affairs. Rabbis are teaching that the Messiah is coming soon and will bring peace to the land. Interest in the Bible is growing among Jews who had considered themselves as "secular". The Jewish people are coming to see that the authentic, Bible loving Christians around the world are their biggest supporters and friends, especially in the United States, which was the first nation to recognize them on May 14, 1948 ,when they declared themselves to be an independent Jewish state, returning to the land promised to them by God to Abraham, Isaac, and Jacob. So far the United States has been a staunch supporter of Israel's right to exist with Jerusalem as their capital, made more affirming by the Trump Administration in 2017 when President Donald Trump announced that the U.S. Embassy, which was located in Tel Aviv, would move to Jerusalem. Trump had been a close ally of the former Israeli Prime Minister, Benjamin Netanyahu and defended him against international hatred and the threats of condemnation by the United Nations, especially from the Muslim nations who are voting members.

There is a new rise in anti-Semitic hostility in the world, calling on nations to boycott Israel, or refer to it as an "apartheid" nation in terms of its relationship with the Palestinians, who see Israel as a nation to be destroyed. More Muslims are entering the U.S. and establishing strongholds in major cities, holding elections for Muslim candidates to become representatives in local, state, and national government. This may cause a coming shift in U.S.- Israeli relations and bring the hatred of the Jews to the minds of the American voting public, who just may call for future governments to break diplomatic relations with Israel and be one more nation to come against God's chosen people as outlined in Scripture (2 Kings 16:6; Esther 3:13; 4:7; 7:4; Psalms 74:8; 83:4; Jeremiah 50:7, 17: Lamentations 4:18; Ezekiel 25:12; 36:3; Daniel 8:24; Acts 16:20; 18:2; 19:34). All it would take is one national election where the forces of socialism and a hatred of God's principles become the national and international policy base that brings this nation to its knees for all time. History warns us, but few tend to listen.

(Sources for this chapter are from notes and statistics on world affairs from a variety of websites such as respective U.S. Government departments and agencies and accumulated data.)

Chapter 11
The Prophecy in the Upper Room

The Synoptic Gospels, the writings of Matthew, Mark, and Luke with their similarities in content and narrative, present the apocalyptic teaching of the Lord Jesus Christ as He met with His disciples on the Mount of Olives. Each gospel tells of troubling and horrific days to come that will affect the entire world and be a visible, unmistakable sign to a wicked humanity that Jesus Christ is returning as the conquering King to reign and rule over a redeemed and renewed earth and people for all time.

The fourth gospel, written by the "beloved apostle" John takes an entirely different course in his recollection of the Lord Jesus. He is not just the promised Messiah but is God Himself come to earth to bring salvation to His people. The first four verses of the first chapter of John present the certainty of Jesus' divine nature as the Creator of all things and was with God the Father from eternity past, with no beginning and no end. As the Divine Creator, He is outside of time, space, and matter and needs nothing to sustain Him. He is self-sufficient, yet loving, caring, and always demonstrating the love of the Father, doing the work that the Father has expected of Him. John records eight miracles that Jesus performed to prove His divinity. Six of these miracles are only found in this gospel. They are the turning of water into wine (2:1-11), the healing of the nobleman's son (4:46-54), the healing of the man at the pool of Siloam (5:1-9), the healing of the man born blind (9:1-7), the raising of Lazarus from the dead (Ch.11), and the quantity of fish caught in the disciple's nets (21:1-6).

Theologian and pastor John MacArthur give John's overall reason for writing his Gospel: **"John is the only one of the four Gospels that contains a precise statement of the author's purpose (20:31). John's objective was both apologetic (defending the faith) and evangelistic. In keeping with his evangelistic purpose, John used the verb "to believe" nearly one hundred times – more than twice as much as the Synoptics, emphasizing that those who believe in Jesus as the Savior will receive eternal life (3:15-16; 4:14; 5:24, 39-40; 6:27, 33, 35,40, 47-48,54, 63, 68; 10:10, 28; 12:50; 14:6; 17:2-3; 20:31). John's evangelistic purpose which is inseparable from his apologetic purpose. He wanted to convince his readers of Jesus' true identity, that of God**

Incarnate (1:1, 14; 8:23, 58; 10:30; 20:28), the Messiah (1:41; 4:25-26), and the Savior of the world (4:42).(The MacArthur New Testament Commentary: John 1-11, Chicago, Moody Press, 2006, p.9)

This chapter is not an overview of the entire gospel. Attention will be focused on the last night Jesus had with His disciples before He was to face betrayal, abandonment, a sham trial, and a horrific death on the cross that would serve an eternal purpose. Chapters 13-17 of John's account take place in what has been referred to as "The Upper Room" (Mark 14:14-15). It would be here where Jesus demonstrated the nature of service, tell of the coming of the Holy Spirit as their teacher and comforter, declare that He alone was the way to God the Father, that He was the vine by which they would bear fruit, look to Him in prayer for their needs in the future, to love one another as He loved them, established the sacrament of communion as a testimony of faith and remembrance to Him, and giving the high priestly prayer on their behalf and of those who come to believe in the future.

In the middle of these teachings, Jesus tells them that He will come again at a future time to receive them to Himself and bring them to heaven. The Scriptures give this account in John 14:1-3: **"Let not your heart be troubled; believe in God, believe also in Me. In My Father's house are many dwelling places. If it were not so, I would have told you, for I go to prepare a place for you. And if I go and prepare a place for you, I will come again and receive you to Myself, that where I am, there you may be also." (NASB).** There are some Bible scholars who claim that these verses are a teaching of the imminent eschatological event known as "the Rapture", defined in a brief manner as **"The snatching of the church out of the world by Christ as presented in 1 Thessalonians 4:13-18." (MacArthur, John. Christ's Prophetic Plans. Chicago: Moody Press, 2012., p.209).** A detailed definition was presented several decades ago by the late Dr. Lewis Sperry Chafer, the founder and first President of Dallas Theological Seminary. In his textbook on doctrine entitled **Major Bible Themes,** he described the Rapture event as follows: **"This event – nowhere dated in the prophecies of the Old Testament – describes the dramatic removal of the church from the earth as the dead in Christ are raised and living Christians are caught up to heaven without dying (1 Corinthians 15:51-58; 1 Thessalonians 4:13-18). This event will bring to a close the purpose of God in terms of the church as a separate company of saints, and the departure of the church will set the stage for the major events leading up to the Second**

Coming of Christ to the earth to set up His millennial kingdom." (Chafer, Lewis Sperry, and Walvoord, John. Major Bible Themes. Grand Rapids, Zondervan, 1974, Revised Edition, p.314).

The Rapture is a coming literal event mentioned in Scripture. As far as it pertains to the study and certainty of prophecy, it must be an actual event scheduled to appear at a given time. It is not to be interpreted as an allegory or mystical term generally referring to the Second Coming. The issue is whether the Rapture event is being described by Jesus in the first three verses of Chapter 14. If it is, then the revelation Paul received from Him that would be written to the church at Thessalonica is sure to happen and be a means of comfort to a troubled people. The late prophecy scholar and pastor Dr. Tim LaHaye, who was also the co-writer of the **Left Behind** series of novels, teamed up with Dr. Ed Hindson of Liberty University to put together a well-written collection of information on end-time events entitled **The Popular Encyclopedia of Bible Prophecy,** published in 2004. In their studies, they each concluded that what the Lord Jesus spoke of in John 14:1-4 did refer to the Rapture event, and not just the assurance of His return alone. Hindson and LaHaye state:

"John 14:1-3 refers to Christ's coming again. It is not a promise to all believers that they will go to Him at death. Rather, it refers to the Rapture of the church. Note the close parallels between the promises of John 14:1-3 and 1 Thessalonians 4:13-18. First, consider the promises of a presence with Christ (14:3) and 1 Thessalonians 4:17. Second, note the promises of comfort (14:1) and that of 4:18 in 1 Thessalonians. Jesus instructed the disciples that He was going to His Father's house (heaven) to prepare a place for them. He promised them that He would return and receive them so that they could be with Him wherever He was." (Hindson, Ed and LaHaye, Tim. The Popular Encyclopedia of Bible Prophecy. Eugene, Oregon. Harvest House Publishers, 2004, pp. 312-313).

Drs. LaHaye and Hindson also produced a companion book to the previous cited source entitled **Exploring Bible Prophecy from Genesis to Revelation (2006).** This work gives an overview of all prophetic verses, events, and the individuals who played their respective role in the history and world of Scripture. They presented an interpretation of John 14:1-6 that tends to supplement their previous conclusions:

"In John 14:1-6, Jesus describes the rapture and the promise of our future home with Him. Though the disciples did not experience the rapture, that does not mean Jesus was wrong. His words apply to a future generation of believers who will go to heaven and not face death. When Christ left earth, it was "to prepare a place for you" in heaven (v.2). He promised to come again "and receive you to Myself, that where I am, there you may be also" (v.3).

"This is the first prediction of the fact that Jesus will return to earth to take believers home with Him to the Father's house (heaven). Meanwhile, until that day, the apostles and other believers are to serve the LORD and testify of the grace of God in the salvation provided by Christ's death, burial, and resurrection." (Hindson, Ed and LaHaye, Tim (Ed.) Exploring Bible Prophecy from Genesis to Revelation. Eugene, Oregon, Harvest House, 2006, p.364)

Television commentator and former Professor of International Law Dr. David Reagan, who is also a noted authority on Bible prophecy, agrees with the interpretation of John 14:1-3 given by Hindson and LaHaye and wrote an article for Lamplighter magazine, a product of **Lamb and Lion** Ministries expressing this agreement. Dr. Reagan's studies and research concluded that these verses spoke of the Rapture event, saying that it was a clear reference spoken of by the Lord Jesus as He prepared His disciples for what was to come.(www.christinprophecy.org/articles/the-rapture. **Accessed May 12, 2020).**

Dr. Thomas Constable, Professor Emeritus of Bible Interpretation at Dallas Seminary and the author of a collection of online expository notes on the books of the Bible declared that the verses spoken by the LORD were referring to a "catching away" of His followers at a certain point in history, interpreted as the Rapture. He wrote in his exposition of John 14:1-3:

"Since Jesus spoke of returning from heaven to take believers there, the simplest explanation seems to be that He was referring to an eschatological return (Acts 1:11). Though these men undoubtedly did not realize it at the time, Jesus was speaking about His return for them at the Rapture rather than His return at the Second Coming. This conclusion is accepted by both pre-tribulation and post-tribulation adherents as a reference to the Rapture." (www.studylight.org/commentaries/dcc. **Accessed May 12, 2002)**

Dr. John Walvoord (1910-2002), late Chancellor, Former President of Dallas Theological Seminary from 1952-1986, and long serving Professor of New Testament Theology was one of the twentieth century's foremost spokesman for the viewpoint of the pre-tribulation Rapture and a defender of the premillennial interpretation of the study of last things (eschatology), was a prolific writer of over fifty books and numerous articles and lectures on the subject of Bible prophecy. He was also an expert in the theological study of Jesus, known as **Christology** and producing a masterful work entitled appropriately **Our Lord Jesus Christ** (1969).

He and an associate named Roy Zuck, who was also a teacher at Dallas Seminary, produced a two- volume work on the Old and New Testaments in 1983 entitled **The Bible Knowledge Commentary.** In the exposition on John, Drs. Walvoord and Zuck, present their respective conclusions on the interpretation of Chapter 14, particularly verses 3-4:

"These respective verses (3-4) refer not to the Resurrection or to a believer's death, but to the Rapture of the church when Christ will return for His people (1 Thess.4:13-18), and they will be with Him. Jesus said nothing about the nature of the place where He was going. It is sufficient that believers will be with the Father and Him (2 Corinthians 5:8; Philippians 1:23; 1 Thessalonians 4:17)" (Walvoord, John F. and Zuck, Roy B. The Bible Knowledge Commentary, New Testament, Vol.2. Wheaton, Illinois, Victor Books, 1983, p.322).

The last entry to make on this subject comes again from the pen of theologian and pastor Dr. John MacArthur, who has been at Grace Community Church in Sun Valley, California since 1969. He undertook a forty- year journey through the New Testament, preaching verse-by-verse and presenting messages that have affirmed the sufficiency of Scripture that have been a means of spiritual maturity and encouragement to all who have heard his teachings over the decades. He has written over one hundred books and Bible studies and is known to be critical of non-biblical precepts within the charismatic movement, along with the present trend of ordaining women pastors, which 1 Timothy 2:12 clearly opposes. He has also addressed in his numerous writings the lack of Biblical support for concepts such as "personal" revelations, signs and wonders, dreams and visions, and the antics of televangelists. Scripture is sufficient for the matters of the church and the individual believer and nothing else needs to be added or deferred from them. He has written commentaries on the entire New Testament, with some books taking up multiple volumes, such as the rich theological treasure that make up the Gospel of John. In his exposition of Chapter 14, he presents the Lord Jesus' assurance to His troubled disciples that while He will leave to return to heaven, He will come again one day to gather His people and bring them to His Father's house. This interpretation is a source of joy to consider, knowing that He has always and will always keep His promises to His elect.

"Jesus' promise, I will come again and receive you to Myself, that where I am, there you may be also, refers to the Rapture of the church (1 Cor. 15:51-54; 1 Thess. 4:13-18; Rev.3:10). The absence of any reference to judgment indicates that the LORD was not referring here to His Second Coming to earth to judge and establish His kingdom (Matthew 13:36-43, 47-50; 24: 29-44; 25:31-46; Rev. 19:11-15), but rather to the catching up of believers into heaven. Further differences between the two events reinforce that truth. At the Second Coming angels gather the elect (Matt.24:30-31), but here Jesus personally told His disciples that He would personally come for them. At the Second Coming the saints will return with Christ (Rev. 19:8, 14) as He comes to set up His earthly kingdom (Rev. 19:11-20:6); here He promises to return for them. Between the Rapture and the Second Coming, the church will celebrate the marriage supper of the Lamb (Rev.19:7-10), and believers will receive their rewards (1 Cor.3:10-15; 4:5; 2 Cor. 5:10). When He returns in judgment and kingdom glory, the saints will come with Him (Rev.19:7, 11-14)." (MacArthur, John. <u>The MacArthur New Testament Commentary: John 12-21.</u> Chicago, Moody Press, 2008, pp.101-102)

There are, doubtless, alternative interpretations of these verses by equally godly expositors of the Scriptures, and viewpoints differ on select passages with the caution about taking a few verses out of a wider context and establishing a teaching or belief that is not in line with orthodox Biblical interpretation. The passage, however one reads and discerns it, emphasizes the fact that Jesus Christ will return one day to make all things new and bring real peace and freedom to the oppressed, forgotten, destitute, and repentant and to usher in a new heaven and earth free from the curse of sin and evil forever (Titus 2:11- 14; Rev. 20:11-15; 21:1-7).To the Christian, there is coming a day of triumph and joy as the Scriptures promise. The tragic fact is, however, the natural man either ignores, dismisses, mocks, or is hostile towards it.This is also a part of prophecy, and it needs to be examined, which will be done in the next chapter.

Chapter 12
Bible Prophecy and Human Nature

The Holy Scriptures have much to say concerning the uniqueness, character, thought, motives, intelligence, and wretched behavior of humanity as we relate to God. The prophecies of Scripture affect all of humanity as either the means of spiritual and national comfort and assurance, as a direct warning of consequences awaiting those who will not bow down and humble themselves before a Holy God, and as the promise of future perfection and wholeness, free from the burdens of sin and rebellion that began in Eden thousands of years ago.

Humanity is the crown jewel of God's creation. We were designed for fellowship and communion with the Creator and given the responsibility of overseeing the entirety of the world, and to live for all time. God put the very essence of life into Adam, making him a living soul, in that the entirety of our design was to be with God in body, mind, and soul (Genesis 1:26-31; 2:7). This personal and unique relationship was shattered by the willful disobedience of the first couple, Adam and Eve. They had listened to the tempting words of the fallen messenger of God who rebelled against Him as well. He is known as Lucifer (light bearer), or Satan (adversary) (Genesis 3; Isaiah 14:7-12; Ezekiel 28:11-15).

It was not long before the wicked rebellious nature of men grew to such a level of depravity that God decided to wipe them off the earth through the deluge (Genesis 6-8). The one man who honored God, Noah, warned the people of what was to come, to no avail (Genesis 6:9; Hebrews 11:7; 2 Peter 2:5). Even after the flood and its aftermath, the descendants of Noah's sons did not heed the lesson of judgment, and sin continued throughout history. We can deny this in order to feel good about ourselves, but Scripture is clear in that we are a wicked, reprobate collection of godless debauchery unable and unwilling to come before God and honor Him in our own strength. We are steeped in sin regardless of what we think, say, or do (Genesis 6:5; Numbers 15:22; 1 Kings 8:46; Job 4:17; Psalm 14:3, 19:12, 53:3, 130:3; Proverbs 20:9; Ecclesiastes 3:16, 7:20; Isaiah 53:6, 64:6; Lamentations 3:39; Daniel 9:11; Micah 7:2; Romans 3:23; Galatians 3:22; 1 John 1:8, 5:19).

In our fallen state, apart from God's mercy and grace, we want nothing to do with Him, preferring our sinful nature and loving it, ignoring the inevitable judgment of God and its eternal, horrendous consequences (Job15:16, 20:12; Psalm 52:3, 62:4; Proverbs 2:14, 5:14; Isaiah 5:18; Jeremiah 5:31, 14:10; Micah 3:2; 2 Thessalonians 2:11-12). We deserve to be judged by God and cast into hell forever for our wickedness, and He would be just and fair for doing so (Psalm 139:8; Matthew 5: 29-30; 10: 15,28; 23:14; 25:41, 46; Luke 16:22-31; Romans 2:8-9; 2 Thessalonians 1:9; Revelation 20:11-15, 21:8). Every page of Scripture presents undeniable evidence and indictment of our vile wickedness, but also proclaim God's mercy, grace, love, and forgiveness if we will repent and turn away from our sins. The Scriptures make it plain that the Sovereign God of all Creation offers His saving grace to anyone. Salvation is of the LORD, and not of our own design (Ex. 14:13; 1 Samuel 2:1; Psalm 14:7, 27:1, 37:39, 62:2, Isaiah 12:2, 25:9; Jeremiah 3:23; Zephaniah 3:17; Ephesians 2:8-9; 1 Timothy 4:10; Revelation 19:1).

Salvation is available from God solely through the Lord Jesus Christ, who came to earth for the purpose of our redemption (Ps. 72:13; Luke 2:11, 19:10; John 3:7; Acts 5:31, 13:23; Romans 8:3; 1 Tim 1:15; 2 Tim 1:10; Hebrews 7:25; 1 John 4:14). He became our substitute, taking our place on the cross as payment for our sins (Ps. 69:9; Isaiah 53:5, 11; 1 Cor.15:3; 2 Cor.5:21; Galatians 3:13; Hebrews 9:28; 1 Peter 2:24, 3:18). The Lord Jesus Christ willfully bore the sins of His people (Leviticus 10:17, 16:22; Numbers 18:1; Isaiah 53:12; Ezekiel 4:5; Heb. 9:28; 1 Peter 2:24; 1 John 3:5). He carried the burdens of many (Genesis 22:6; Isaiah 53:4; Mat. 8:17; John 19:17) and became the sole Mediator between God and humanity (Jer. 18:20; John 14:6; Ephesians 2:18; 1 Timothy 2:5; Heb. 8:6, 9:15, 24, 12:24, 1 John 2:1).

The Lord Jesus was the spotless Lamb of God (Is. 53:7; John 1:29; 1 Cor.5:7; 1 Pet. 1:19; Rev. 5:6, 6:1, 7:9, 12:11, 13:8, 14:1, 15:3, 17:14, 19:9, 21:22), and offered Himself as the final sacrifice for sin (Is. 53:4; John 15;13, 18:14; 2 Cor, 8:9; Gal.1:4; Eph. 5:2; Titus 2:14; Heb. 9:26; 1 Pet.3:18; 1 John 3:16; Rev. 1:5). The suffering and death of the Lord Jesus on the cross redeemed us once and for all (Is. 53:12; John 10:11, 12:23, 24; Rom. 5:6, 14:9; 1 Cor. 15:3; 2 Cor.5:15; Col.1:22; Heb. 2:9; Rev. 5:9). He is the only intercessor (Is. 59:16), the sole remedy for the disease of sin (Jn. 3:14), the sole spiritual nourishment (Jn. 6:35), the only real source of absolute truth

(Jn. 14:6), the only Savior (Acts 4:12), and the only foundation of life (1 Cor. 3:11; Col. 3:11).

So, what does humanity think about this wondrous gift of forgiveness and salvation from the LORD? Many people willfully neglect it to pursue their own selfish interests (Ezek.33:9; Luke 14:18; Acts 24:25, 28:27; Heb. 2:3, 12:25). Others look at God's mercy with an attitude of indifference (Luke 17:16-20; Acts 18:12-16) and hatred (Gen. 26:27; Ex. 20:5; Zech. 11:9; Luke 6:11, 19:14; John 7:7, 15:18, 25, 19:6). The apostle Paul wrote of man's attitude before God's offering of grace and mercy. All people, despite their declaration that there is no God, know deep down that He exists and that they are without excuse (Romans 1:18-20). They tend to fashion their own gods, arrogantly and defiantly worshipping them instead of the Creator (vv.21-23). God is never bothered by this defiance or does He show any worry about being neglected. He brings His judgment on their wickedness and rebellion by giving them up to their sin, which will get worse and more depraved over time. They openly embrace sexual deviancy (vv.26-27), further descending into perverse and evil actions. Their ending comes with shutting out the mercy of God in their lives, willfully accept and practice ever increasing and deviant behavior so much, that they will encourage others to partake in their practices as well (v. 32) and approve of it.

The letter by Paul to the Romans never makes humanity out to be better than what they are in the eyes of God. Everyone, without exception, are wicked and vile in different degrees (3:10-18), and cannot in any way, shape, form, or circumstance ever hope to redeem himself from his sin nature. We all fall short of God's glory because of our sins (3:23). Yet, Paul writes of the hope we have through Jesus Christ (5:6-11). To refuse this hope is to die in your sins (6:23), but if you place your faith in Jesus Christ for salvation, you will no longer be condemned by the sins that kept you imprisoned (8:1). We have the privilege of communicating with God through prayer. When we do not know what to say, it is the Holy Spirit dwelling within us that offers prayer to the Father. The Trinity. (Father, Son, Holy Spirit) aid in our spiritual journey for the remainder of our days and on into eternity. There is absolutely nothing that will separate us from the LORD (8: 31-39). The salvation provided by the finished work of Christ on the cross is available to all who call on Him (10: 8-10, 13). As we mature in the faith, we are to avoid the influence of the world to deter us from remaining close to Christ and to live a life fully dedicated to Him.

Without the conviction of the Holy Spirit, no one comes to Christ, and many people will refuse to bow the knee to Him in this life. As Paul got older and was preparing to hand the reigns of pastoral responsibility to his successors such as Timothy, he wrote of the behavior of unrepentant humanity that would only worsen as the last days approached and of the type of preaching they would approve and enjoy (Mt. 5:19, 15:9, 14; 23:16; 24:23; Luke 6:39; 11:52; 17:23; Acts 15:24; 2 Cor.11:4, 13; Gal. 1:9, 5:8; Phil. 1:15; 1 Tim. 1:7, 4:2, 6:3; 2 Tim. 4:3; Titus 1:11; 2 Peter 2:1; 2 John 10; Rev. 2:2).

The last days will see many people who claim to be saved walk away from the "faith" they never possessed in the first place and will deny Christ (Pr. 30:9; Matt. 10:13, 26:34, 69, 70; Mark 8:38; Acts 3:14; 2 Tim. 2:12; Hebrews 6:4-6; Titus 1:16; 2 Peter 2:1; 1 John 2:22). The letter from Jesus' half-brother Jude speaks of apostates in the church with their deceptiveness and treachery who will lead many astray. (Jude 1-25). In the book of Revelation, we read of unrepentant humanity cursing and blaspheming God among the horrid series of judgments on the earth for its wickedness and evils (6:12-17; 9:1-6, 20; 13:4; 16:1-11; 19:21; 20:11-15).

The message of Scripture is clear. We are born in sin and will die in sin, spending eternity in hell if we do not repent and surrender our lives to the Lord Jesus Christ for forgiveness of sin and salvation, bowing to Him as Lord of our lives and serving Him here and beyond. Rejection of the gift of redemption through Christ alone will send you to hell forever where there is no mercy, grace, love, compassion, joy, rest, comfort, or way out. The prophetic word proclaims this truth as true and absolute. You would be a foolish person not to come to Christ while there is still time (2 Corinthians 6:2; Hebrews 9:27). In surrendering to Him, you will enter the joy of heaven forever, either through death or by the Rapture, which will be the next topic of study.

Chapter 13

The Blessed Hope

This present world is in its final phase. Common sense tells us that the troubles and tragedies we are experiencing, along with the progression of perverse and unnatural behaviors and lifestyles, the mockery and disdain for tradition and conservative values, the increasing corruption of governments around the world, the rise of natural disasters, and general uneasiness felt by nearly everyone are not what this world should consider as normal and acceptable. Something has got to give. We have reached a moral and ethical tipping point where the solution will come from a call for and return to absolute moral standards based on traditional Judeo-Christian traditions, or we will surely fall into a rapid and unstoppable descent, taking this nation and world further into chaos and anarchy, leading to the end of civilization as we know it.

The Christian worldview has all but disappeared from American life. Much of the organized church has bent over backward to accommodate people who do not have any interest in conforming to the demands of the Gospel. They instead want to be a part of the congregation without being expected to change their behavior and lifestyle and surrender all to Christ. We are becoming an enemy of the state as the days pass, and open hostility to the message of Christ is more obvious. There are national, state, and local governing authorities who would love to see the Christians incarcerated, driven out of society, shut down, silenced, or worse. We have witnessed in the past few years the slaughter and displacement of believers in the Middle East under the brutal hand of radical jihadists like ISIS, Boko Haram, Al Qaeda, the Taliban, and forces in Egypt and Syria. These brethren have been ignored for the most part by the world system and previous administrations of nations. The true remnant church is weary and anxious to be with the LORD. We have run out of energy, so to speak, and we have faced the enemy continually in one form or another. In our look at John 14:1-3, we are assured by the Lord Jesus that He is coming back to receive us and take us to our home in heaven. He promised His disciples and all who would come to Him in the years ahead that He would return. Many of us are saying quietly and openly, "Any time now, LORD. I'm ready to go." The Scriptures tell us that this promise is not far off, and it has been known by many believers as the Rapture, defined as: **"God suddenly taking up the church from earth to heaven at the first part of Christ's second coming."** (Hindson, Ed, and LaHaye Tim. <u>The Popular Encyclopedia of Bible Prophecy.</u> Eugene, OR, Harvest House, 2004, p. 311).

The Scriptures that are associated with the event of the Rapture are John 14:1-3, which was covered in a previous chapter. The apostle Paul wrote letters to the churches he had founded in the cities of Corinth and Thessalonica on his second missionary journey around A.D.49-51. He had written a previous letter to the church at Galatia in approximately A.D. 48 and is considered by Bible experts to be the first letter in what would become the New Testament Canon.

Corinth was a city with a bad reputation, even for Rome's deviant tastes. In the introduction to his commentary on 1 Corinthians, Dr. John MacArthur gives a condensed overview of the city's numerous sins: **"Even to the pagan world the city was known for its moral corruption, so much that in classical Greek the term "to behave like a Corinthian" came to represent gross immorality and drunken debauchery. The name of the city became synonymous with moral depravity. In this letter to the church there, Paul lists some of the city's characteristic sins – fornication, idolatry, effeminacy, homosexuality, stealing, covetousness, drunkenness, abusive speech, and swindling. Some of the Corinthian believers had been guilty of practicing these sins before their conversion and had been cleansed (6:11). Others in the church, (reminds them even pagan Gentiles did not commit, such as incest (5:1)."** (MacArthur, John. <u>The MacArthur New Testament Commentary: 1 Corinthians</u>. Chicago, Moody Press, 1984, p. viii). Other commentators on the reprobate mindset of Corinth have presented a similar view.

1 Corinthians 15 begins with a discourse on the resurrection of Jesus and its centrality to the faith. Paul affirms that Jesus died for our sins and was raised from the dead according to the Scriptures. Simon Peter was the first apostle to see Him. He then appeared to the other apostles and was seen by over five hundred eyewitnesses who could be contacted for verification, although some had already passed away. His half-brother James saw Him, as well by the apostles for a second time. He last appeared to Paul, who considered himself unworthy of an honor and calling in being chosen for apostleship (vv.8-11; 1 Timothy 1:12-17). He continues to argue the point

that if Jesus was still dead, then we are without hope and dead in our sins, lost forever. The chapter concludes with the following verses: "Behold, I tell you a mystery: We shall not all sleep, but we shall all be changed – in a moment, in the twinkling of an eye, at the last trumpet. For the trumpet shall sound, and the dead will be raised incorruptible, and we shall be changed. For this corruptible must put on incorruption, and this mortal must put on immortality. So, when this corruptible has put on incorruption, and this mortal shall put in immortality, then shall be brought to pass the saying that is written, 'Death is swallowed up in victory. O Death, where is your sting? O grave, where is your victory?"1 Corinthians 15:51-55)

W. Harold Mare, contributing writer on 1 Corinthians for the **Expositor's Bible Commentary,** gives a well-organized summary of Paul's teaching on the resurrection: **"God's people must have more than the natural body to inherit the eternal kingdom of God. This mortal body is perishable and cannot inherit that which is imperishable. So, the unsaved cannot be in heaven at all, and the saved must have their bodies changed. In referring to the resurrection body, Paul implies that there are various things about that body which the Corinthians did not understand, and about which he wants to inform them. Not all Christians will fall asleep, for some will be live when Christ returns (1 Thess. 4:17). All Christians will receive changed bodies when Christ comes back and summons His people at the sound of the last trumpet (Rev.11:15). The change will occur instantaneously and completely for all Christians, living or dead. We will receive "imperishable" bodies like Christ's. Death has no sting of finality, and the grave has no victory." (Mare, W. Harold, in The Expositor's Bible Commentary, Vol. 2, New Testament Grand Rapids, Zondervan, 1994, p.654).**

David K. Lowery, Professor of New Testament Exegesis at Dallas Theological Seminary, a contributor to the **Bible Knowledge Commentary,** wrote of 15:51-55: **"Paul had revealed the same truth to the Thessalonians (1 Thess. 4:15-17). The rapture of the church was a mystery in that it had not been known in the Old Testament but was now revealed. The dead in Christ will first be raised, and then the living will be instantaneously transformed. The trumpet, as in the Old Testament, signaled the appearance of God (Ex. 19:16). It is the last blast for the church because this appearance will never end. Like the dead, the living will exchange the temporal and imperfect for the** eternal and perfect. For those who belong to Christ, death's power shall be removed." (Lowery, David K. "1 Corinthians" in The Bible Knowledge Commentary, Vol. 2. Wheaton, Ill., 1983, pp.545-546).

Ed Hindson and Tim LaHaye, whose works have been cited in earlier studies, give their respective insight on the teaching of Paul concerning the importance of the resurrection: **"In these verses and in 1 Thessalonians 4:13-18, the apostle Paul mentions both the resurrection and the "change" that describes the rapture of the church. The rapture is also called a "mystery" that has to do with the fact that "we shall not all sleep, but we will all be changed" (15:51). This great event was not revealed in the Old Testament. First Corinthians 15:52 is virtually the same as 1 Thessalonians 4:16-17, which is a well- known rapture passage." There the trumpet is sounded and the resurrection of the dead in Christ takes place. Then the believers who are alive on earth "shall be caught up together with them to meet the LORD in the air." The "change" takes place followed by the catching up. This is the imparting of the new, heavenly, glorious body Paul taught about." (Exploring Bible Prophecy from Genesis to Revelation, p. 415).**

The godly men listed here who have dedicated their lives and minds to study and teach the riches of the Word of God are in agreement with the belief that 1 Corinthians 15:51-54 is a reference to the time of the rapture of the church. Other scholars may respectfully differ as to interpretation, but there is a consensus among believers that these verses are dealing specifically with the last days before the promised return of the Lord Jesus Christ. These verses are also a reliable source of evidence against skeptical thought that denies or doubts the possibility of life after death. This was a point of contention and debate among the Greek and Roman philosophers of Paul's day. He dealt with this and other issues while in Athens, presenting the case for Jesus Christ before the philosophers at Mars Hill (Acts 17:16-34).

We now turn our attention towards those Scriptures that clearly present the rapture as an inevitable literal event in history. It will involve all true believers in Jesus Christ and will be an immediate occurrence that will usher in the destruction of this fallen world, its evil systems, and the deceptive work and words of the devil, and forever establish the righteous rule of the Lord Jesus Christ upon a new heaven and earth, free from the curse of sin and death for all eternity. We will now study 1 Thessalonians and the wondrous promise Paul gave to a young church going through intense persecution. John Walvoord, in his book **Every Prophecy of the Bible**

(1999) gives his readers an overview of the church and the letters sent to it in their time of trouble:

"Probably the first of Paul's inspired epistles, 1 Thessalonians has a special place in that it was addressed to a young church. Paul founded this church on his second missionary journey when he spent three Sabbath days preaching the Gospel. Though the Jews who rejected Paul's message and stirred up trouble and forced Paul to leave, the young Christians in Thessalonica stood firm and formed the nucleus of the church there. To encourage them in their faith, Paul wrote his two epistles to them. Especially significant is the fact that the doctrine of the coming of the LORD and related events form one of the main doctrines in both 1 and 2 Thessalonians with some reference to the coming of the LORD in every chapter. The instruction given by Paul in the field of prophecy was the basis for the teaching in his epistles. Especially significant is the detailed account of the Rapture in 4:13-18." (Walvoord, John. Every Prophecy of the Bible. Colorado Springs, Chariot Victor Publishers, 1999, p.478).

Historical research and the work of archaeologists specializing in the periods of the Greek and Roman empires has been going on since the 19th century, beginning with the work of Heinrich Schliemann (1822-1890) who undertook a quest to locate the city of Troy, which had been mentioned in the works of the Greek poet Homer (800's B.C.) and centered on the saga of the Trojan Wars. Contemporary thinking was that the city of Troy, like most of the events in Homer's epic poem, was fiction. Schliemann thought otherwise and traveled to Greece to examine the areas the poem had mentioned and started to carefully excavate the area where Homer had placed the city's location. With a copy of The Odyssey as his guide, he discovered the existence of Troy exactly where Homer had mentioned it and discovered that the ruins of five other cities were built on top of the original settlement. His work won him worldwide accolade in the field of historical scholarship, and became a major influence on international exploration, forensic science and initiated archaeological expeditions throughout the world, resulting in major discoveries such as the central American pyramids, the mountain city of Machu Pichu, and similar finds in other areas of Central and South America by scientists and explorers such as Hiram Bingham (1875-1956) and Sir Percy Fawcett (1867-1925)

The science of Egyptology, based on the discovery and research of ancient tombs and exploration of sites such as the Giza Pyramids, the ruins of cities like Luxor, Ramses, Thebes, and Memphis were undertaken by British archaeologists such as the brilliant yet eccentric Sir Flinders Petrie (1853-1942), who accurately measured and explored the Great Pyramid of Cheops. Howard Carter (1874-1939), became renowned worldwide for discovering the tomb of King Tutankhamen in 1924.Sir Arthur Evans (1881-1941) had explored the island of Crete and discovered the ruins of the palace of King Minos near the city of Knossos as well as engravings of symbols of a primitive language that Evans would refer to as "Linear B". It would be the foundation of the Greek alphabet written and used in the establishment of city-states such as Athens and Sparta and would be the foundation of classical Greek culture.

Dr. David Livingstone, a medical missionary (1813-1873) not only spread the gospel to the populations of equatorial Africa but discovered what would be come to known as Victoria Falls and the source of the Nile River. Sir Leonard Wooley (1880-1960) worked on excavations in Mesopotamia (Iraq) and the area known as Ur of the Chaldees, which was the ancestral home of the patriarch Abraham (Genesis 12-25). The late 19th century also saw the origins of archaeological expeditions begin in Greece, which had recently won its independence from the grip of the Ottoman Turks in 1850 who before had made it a part of its vast Middle Eastern Empire.

The Ottomans had destroyed the last remaining vestiges of the Byzantine (Eastern Roman) Empire in 1453 which had been established in 315 A.D. under the reign of Constantine, the first "Christian" emperor of Rome. It had lasted for over a thousand years until the fall and subsequent looting of the capital, Constantinople. The Byzantine empire took upon itself the task of being both the collectors and guardians of numerous manuscripts of the Christian Scriptures from centuries past and became a hub of Christian mission work. They originated and developed the idea of allowing their imperial subjects basic legal rights and protections, first enacted by Emperor Justinian I (527-565). This would be carried over eventually into the developing European nations that came into being after the fall of the Western Roman Empire in A.D. 476

This "Code of Justinian" was known as **common law** and a foundation of the English parliamentary system that began with the signing of the **Magna Carta** by King John in 1215 A.D. Future parliaments in English history would place limits on the powers of the Monarch and be the actual ruling authority of the nation. The parliamentary system would become be the forerunner for the development of representative government in America. For this and other ideas, western civilization is indebted to the Greek and Roman Empires for the development of philosophical and political concepts, and were advocates of advanced mathematics, mechanics, science, law, the arts, language, logic and critical thinking,

There were serious issues facing the churches established by Paul and his associates on the missionary journeys recorded in the book of Acts. One had erupted in the church that Paul had established in Thessalonica. In his book **Archaeology and the New Testament,** Dr. John McKay, Professor Emeritus of New Testament at Wheaton College (Ph.D., University of Chicago) describes the city's historical significance within the Empire: **"Paul's arrival in Thessalonica (Acts 17:1) put him in the capital city of the second district of Macedonia, and from the time of Pompey, the seat of the governor of the entire province. Placed under senatorial jurisdiction in A.D. 44, the metropolis enjoyed the status of "civitas libera", or "free city", as well. Under the emperor Claudius (A.D. 41-54), coins were first minted in Macedonia, so prosperity was everywhere evident about the time Paul arrived in the late fall of 49. Among the first Thessalonian converts were "Greek women of high standing", who took their place in a society that boasted great families possessing enormous wealth. Indications of such prosperous families has been found at Thessalonica, Berea, and Philippi." (Published by Baker Academic, Grand Rapids, MI, pp.292 -293).**

Paul had taught the new believers in Thessalonica that Jesus Christ was the true Savior of humanity, proclaimed by the prophets of the Old Testament and were taught to the Jews who worshipped in the local synagogues. The proofs of miracles, teachings and redemptive work of the Lord Jesus were spread by the apostles and those who had been discipled by them. There was the testimony of Paul himself who had been a persecutor of the Christians before his own encounter and commission by the risen Christ on the road to Damascus (Acts 9). His missionary work was not without hardship (2 Corinthians 11:22-33), but the result was the spread of the Gospel throughout the Roman Empire within thirty years after Christ's ascension (Acts 1:1-11).A key doctrine was the fact that Jesus would return for His people. However, some were concerned that their loved ones who had come to Christ and then died would be left behind at the time of the

120

rapture. False teachers had sown confusion after Paul had been forced to leave the city by non-believing Jews and pagan citizens. Paul heard of this confusion and upon hearing a direct word from the LORD Himself, wrote to explain the truth of what would happen at the time of Jesus' return and bring His people to their real home in heaven.

The order of events that will signal the Rapture (the catching away of the remnant church) is listed in 4:13-18:

"But I do not want you to be ignorant, brethren, concerning those who have fallen asleep, lest you sorrow as others who have no hope. For if we believe that Jesus died and rose again, even so God will bring with Him those who sleep in Jesus. For this we say to you by the word of the LORD, that we who are alive and remain until the coming of the LORD will by no means precede those who are asleep. For the LORD Himself will descend from heaven with a shout, with the voice of the archangel, and with the trumpet of God, and the dead in Christ will rise first. Then we who are alive and remain shall be caught up with them in the clouds to meet the LORD in the air and then we shall always be with the LORD. Therefore comfort one another with these words." (NKJV)

John MacArthur wrote in his commentary on 1 Thessalonians a basic explanation of what will occur:

- The LORD Himself will return for His church.

- Jesus will descend from heaven.

- He will do so with a shout.

- The voice of the archangel will sound.

- The trumpet of God will be heard.

- The dead in Christ will rise first.

- The believers who are alive will be taken up to meet the LORD in the air, where we will always be with Him and receive our new glorified bodies.

Dr. MacArthur, and other like-minded biblical prophecy teachers tend to believe in and teach that the Rapture will occur before the time of great tribulation upon the world is unleashed by God as judgment for the wickedness, blasphemy, and reprobation of humanity who refuse to accept Jesus' offer of salvation and mercy. This time of horrific circumstances is described in detail in the book of Revelation, which in and of itself takes up an entire volume and will not be addressed in this work. Dr. Mac Arthur presents his reasons why he advocates a pre-tribulation rapture:

- First, the earthly kingdom of Christ promised in Revelation 6-18 does not mention the church as being on Earth.

- Revelation 19 does not mention a Rapture even though that is where a post-tribulation Rapture (if true) would logically appear. Thus, one can conclude that the Rapture will have already occurred.

- A post-tribulation Rapture renders the entire concept itself inconsequential. If God preserves the church during the Tribulation as post-tribulation supporters assert, then why have it at all?

- If God raptures and glorifies all believers just prior to the inauguration of the millennial kingdom, as a post-tribulation Rapture demands, no one would be left to populate and propagate the earthly kingdom of Christ promised to Israel.

- The New Testament does not warn of an impending tribulation such as is experienced during Daniel's seventieth week, for church age believers. It does warn of error and false prophets (Acts 20:29-30; 2 Peter 2:1; 1 John 4:13), against ungodly living (Eph. 4:25-5:7) and present troubles (1 Thess. 2:14-16; 2 Peter). It would make no sense then for the Scriptures to be silent concerning such a traumatic time of history if the post-tribulation position was true.

- Paul's instructions to the Thessalonians demand a pre-tribulation Rapture because if he were teaching a post-tribulation view, the living saints would rejoice that their deceased loved ones in the LORD would be spared the approaching horrors. However, they were not in a state of dread by reading Paul's letter but were given hope and a sense of joy due to the belief of being caught up before the tribulation.

- The sequence of events at Christ's coming line up with a pre-tribulation Rapture event. The Rapture and the Second Coming are two separate events:

- At the Rapture, Jesus gathers His own (4:16-17). Angels gather the elect at the Second Coming (Matt. 24:31)

- At the Rapture, resurrection is prominent (4:15-16). Scripture does not mention resurrection at the Second Coming.

- At the Rapture, Christ comes to reward believers (4:17). At the Second Coming, He judges the earth (Matt.25:31-46).

- At the Rapture, the true believers are taken from the earth (4:15-17). At the Second Coming, He takes away unbelievers (Matt.24:37-41)

- Unbelievers remain on earth after the Rapture, while believers remain on the earth at the Second Coming.

- Concerning the Rapture, Jesus does not come to establish His kingdom, whereas He does so at His Second Coming.

- Believers receive glorified bodies at the Rapture, while no one receives new bodies at the Second Coming.

- Some of Jesus' own parables give evidence of a pre-tribulation Rapture, such as the wheat and tares (Matt. 13:24-30), the dragnet (13:47-50), and the days of Noah and impending judgment as presented in the Olivet Discourse (Mat. 24-26).

- Revelation 3:10 teaches that the Lord Jesus will remove the true church prior to the Tribulation. The church will not go through the hour of testing that will come upon the earth. From these presentations, it would be logical to assume that the position of the pre-tribulation Rapture makes the most sense. **(MacArthur, 1 Thessalonians, pp.133-137)**

While the predominant belief of many prophecy teachers tend to support the idea of a pre-tribulation Rapture, there are others who advocate that Christians will go through the time of the Great Tribulation but be spared God's judgment and wrath that will be poured out on the rebellious earth.

Others teach that we will be raptured at the mid-point of the Tribulation and be spared the final judgments. There was a brief movement of what was referred to as the "pre-wrath" Rapture several years ago but has lost any real support. Some have taught that only those who have seriously looked for the time of the Rapture will be taken and those Christians who had not lived a worthy life will be left behind. Much of this mindset is based on the thought that our brethren in the past were not spared persecution, so why should this generation be any different?

Others believe that going through the Tribulation will somehow "purify" the church from its faults. Some brave souls are convinced that they will go through the Tribulation to prove a point that they can endure what is to come for the glory of God and to demonstrate their faith and belief. It would be in our best interest and for the sake of fairness to look at these beliefs in more detail. Dr. Ron Rhodes, the founder of <u>Reasoning Through the Scriptures</u>, an evangelistic and apologetic ministry, is also a noted author, having written several books on prophecy and studies of books of the Bible. In one of his recent releases, entitled <u>The End Times in Chronological Order</u> (2012), he writes a brief description of each view:

- **Post-Tribulation View:** Bible expositors George Eldon Ladd, Robert Gundry, and Irvin Baxter hold to this interpretation. They believe that Christ will rapture the church at the Second Coming, meaning that the church will go through the time of the Tribulation as given in the book of Revelation, but will be protected from the wrath of Satan during this period. This presents a dilemma in interpretation, such as the promise given to the church in Revelation 3:10. Using texts such as Matthew 24:7-9 and Revelation 20:4-6, they support their argument that the church will go through this terrible period of prophetic history. Pre-tribulation supporters present the existence of believers referred to as "tribulation saints", those who come to Christ during the Tribulation and risk being executed for their faith (Revelation 7:9-17). As stated earlier in this chapter, the idea of a pre-tribulation Rapture seems to have a more logical and orderly flow of events than what has been presented by post-tribulation adherents.

- **The Mid-Tribulation Viewpoint:** This is the belief that Christians will endure the first half of the Tribulation, and then be taken from the earth by the LORD before the second half of the Tribulation starts, which, according to Scripture (Matthew 24:15-

28; Mark 13:14-23; Luke 17:23-24, 37: 21:20-24; Revelation, Chs.15, 16) is far worse than what has already taken place. This was taught by proponents as Gleason Archer (1916-2004), J. Oliver Boswell (1895-1977), and Merrill Tunney (1904-1983) A more detailed survey is presented in Dr. Pentecost's **Things to Come** (pp. 179-192) and is worth examining, although he makes it clear that he is a proponent of the pre-tribulation view.

- **The Partial Rapture View:** This view has very few proponents but was taught by in the writings of Witness Lee (1905-1977), based upon a questionable exposition of the Parable of the Ten Virgins (Matthew25:1-13) where five were prepared and five were not, signifying that faithful Christians will be taken away, while the unfaithful will be left behind to suffer through the Tribulation. Beyond this passage of Scripture, there are no others to confirm this view.

- **Pre-Wrath Rapture:** This view, proposed by Marvin Rosenthal and Robert Van Kampen received a period of attention in the mid-1990's as a counterargument to the pre-tribulation position. It taught that the church will not be raptured until the sixth and seventh trumpets of judgment (Revelation 6:12-8:1) are poured on the earth, which is the concluding of all judgment on the earth by the LORD. This view never caught on with prophecy teachers or many believers and faded out quickly. **(Rhodes, Ron. The End Times in Chronological Order. Eugene, OR., Harvest House, 2012, pp.50-53)**

There is an erroneous teaching in some end-time circles who teach that the church will undergo the period of the Great Tribulation in order to be "purged" and "cleansed" before it is ready to become the Bride of Christ. The origins of such a view are not from any one specific teacher or denomination, but it is an interpretation that seems to be an extreme form of the post-tribulation rapture position, as if the grace and mercy of Christ are not enough. This view is borderline heresy, daring to suggest that we go through a type of "purgatory" before the LORD approves of our walk with Him. This is nothing but a form of "works-based" salvation, part of not only Roman Catholic theology, but also the basis for pseudo-Christian "cults" such as Mormonism and Jehovah's Witnesses. It goes against Scriptures like Matthew 11:28-30; Romans 5:6-11; 8:31-39; Ephesians 2:8-9 and Galatians 1:8-9. We add nothing to our salvation, it is of the LORD

(Ps. 37:39; John 10:9, 14:6; Acts 4:12, 15:11; Romans 5:9; 1 Thess.5:9). Rest assured that our Lord Jesus will never leave or forsake us, and that He has us in His hand, and no one can remove us from Him (John 10:28-30; Hebrews 13:5).

Chapter 14

Historical and Theological Confessions in Respect to the End Times

As Christianity spread throughout the Roman Empire and to other lands in the course of history, there would also be an equally determined effort of those opposed to the gospel of Christ to present counterfeit doctrines and teachings that were in direct violation of the instructions and writings of the apostles and the church fathers who had been their disciples. The Lord Jesus had told His disciples in the Olivet Discourse that false teachers would appear on the scene, ready to deceive anyone who would hear them out and end up following a lie that resembled the truth of God's Word (Isaiah 5:20, 9:16, 43:27; Jeremiah 23:17, 23:24, 28:16, 29:32; Ezekiel 13:7; Matt. 5:19, 15:9, 14; 23:16; 24:23; Luke 6;39, 11:52, 17:23; Acts 15:24; 2 Cor.11:4, 13; Gal. 1:8-9, 5:8; Phil.1;15; 1 Tim.1:7, 4:2; 6:3; 2 Tim.4:3; Titus 1:11; 2 Pet.2:1; 2 John 1:10; Rev.2:2).

 Scripture goes on to specify the traits of these agents of deception and evil, and their sinister presence even more so in these last days before the return of the Lord Jesus Christ. They are perverters of God's grace (Gal.1:6-8), lovers of money (Luke 16:14), deniers of the person and work of Christ (2 Peter 2:1), oppressors of the truth of the Gospel (2 Tim. 3:8), spreaders of myths and forgeries (2 Tim. 4:3, 4). They are deprivers of the truth (1 Tim. 6:3-5), wrapped up in traditions (Matt. 15:9), are unstable (1 Tim. 1:6,7), deceitful (Eph.4:14), and are bound in lust (2 Peter 2:12-19).

False teachers have been pebbles in the shoes of the gospel of peace since Pentecost (acts 2:1-39; 20:28-30; Eph. 6:10-18). They were a source of trouble for Paul and his companions in ministry (2 Tim. 1:14, 15), and even more so with this age (1 Tim. 4:1-3) as the return of Christ grows more imminent (1 Tim. 4:3-4). The Bible never shies away from naming them, as we should in these times. There was the greedy prophet Balaam (Rev. 2:14), the sorcerer bar-Jesus (Acts 13:6), the negligent elders of Ephesus (Rev.2:2), the hedonistic Epicurean philosophers (Acts 17:18), false apostles (2 Cor. 11:5, 13, 12:11), the secular Jews who supported Herod (Mark 3:6, 12:13), the Sadducees (Matt. 16:12), the Pharisees (Matt. 23: 26), and the instigator himself, Satan, who started the deception in Eden (Gen. 3:4).

In the period of church history after the beginning and spread of the Protestant Reformation initiated by men of God such as Martin Luther (1483-1546), John Calvin (1509-1564), John Knox of Scotland (1514-1572), Bishop Hugh Latimer of England (1487-1555), and Ulrich Zwingli of Basel, Switzerland (1484-1531), the concepts of Scriptural authority, faith alone, grace alone, Christ alone, and all glory to God alone spread throughout Europe and Great Britain. Bibles were printed in the language of the people and the Gospel was taken to the New World during the ages of the Renaissance and Exploration. Godly ministers within the movement also felt that it was necessary to put together a series of beliefs and standards that would be used by the Protestant congregations as a way of teaching not just the Scriptures, but the essential doctrines as well.

In 1647 a group of Puritan ministers and scholars gathered in order to produce a comprehensive list of Biblical and doctrinal standards. The result was the **Westminster Confession of Faith**, used by Reformed and Presbyterian Church and was the inspiration for works such as the **1689 Baptist Confession of Faith,** which was similar in all the doctrines save for the ordinance of baptism. The Presbyterians and other Reformed congregations practiced infant baptism, while the Baptists taught baptism by immersion upon a confession of salvation in Christ. The 1689 Confessions and doctrinal questions, known as the **catechism,** was adopted by the Baptists who came to America in the late 1700's and began preaching to settlers who were heading to new territories beyond the established colonies.

In 1845, members of Baptist churches in the South took issue with Northern Baptist congregations over slavery and increasing progressive thought. They broke away and formed the denomination known today as the **Southern Baptist Convention**. As the denomination grew and expanded throughout the nation, it adopted the 1689 Confession as well, but in later years, most notably after the beginning of the twentieth century, doctrines such as divine election were minimized and an emphasis on evangelism and missions took shape. In 1963 a new version of the 1925 confession was written and approved by the delegates at the annual convention. It became known as **The Baptist Faith and Message** and was promoted by pastors such as Herschel Hobbs (1907-1995) and W.A. Criswell (1909-2002), becoming the standard for SBC churches until a revision in 2000 was adopted that added a section on the family and its importance.

Each of these confessions and statement of beliefs contain a section on the doctrine of last things, avoiding prophetic interpretations and sequences that were being taught by pastors who had a premillennial point of view such as William Bell Riley (1863-1947), Frank Norris (1870-1952), R.A. Torrey (1856-1928), Donald Grey Barnhouse (1895-1960), and the emerging fundamentalist movement led by John R. Rice (1895-1980). Most SBC leaders and pastors were amillennial in their views or chose not to address the issue in sermons and teachings. Noted pastors such as George W. Truett (1867-1944) of the First Baptist Church of Dallas never mentioned end-time issues in any sermon during his forty -year long tenure. His successor, Dr. W.A. Criswell (1909-1992), was a proponent of the pre-tribulation rapture, and made the doctrine of premillennialism more popular and accepted in the SBC over the decades. These confessions and statements of faith have everything to do with the study of Biblical prophecy. Knowledge of Scripture and doctrine keeps you safe from deception.

The Westminster Confession of Faith (1647)

Chapter XXXII

Of the State of Men after Death, and of the Resurrection of the Dead

- The bodies of men, after death, return to dust, and see corruption, but their souls, which neither die nor sleep, having an immortal substance immediately return to God who gave them. The souls of the righteous, being then made perfect in holiness are received into the highest heavens, where they behold the face of God in light and glory, waiting for the redemption of their bodies. The souls of the wicked are cast into hell where they remain in torments and utter darkness, reserved to the judgment of the great day. Besides these two places, for souls separated from their bodies, the Scriptures acknowledge none. (Eccl. 12:7; Luke 12:13, 16:23,23:43; John 18:36; Gen. 3:19; Acts 1:25, 3:21, 13:36; Heb. 12:33; 2 Cor.5:1; Phil. 1:23; Eph.4:10: Jude 6; 1 Peter 3:19).

- At the last day, such as are found alive shall not die, but be changed, and all the dead shall be raised up with the selfsame bodies, and none other (although with different qualities), which shall be united with their souls forever (1 Thess. 4:17; 1 Cor. 15:42,51; Job 19:26).

- The bodies of the unjust shall, by the power of Christ, be raised to dishonor. The bodies of the just, by His Spirit, unto honor and be made conformable to His own glorious body (Acts 24:15; John 5:28;1 Cor.15:43; Phil.3:21).

Chapter XXXIII

Of the Last Judgment

- God has appointed a day wherein He will judge the world in righteousness by Jesus Christ to whom all power and judgment is given of the Father. In that day, the apostate angels will be judged, but likewise all persons that have lived upon earth shall appear before the tribunal of Christ to give an account of their thoughts, words, and deeds. They will receive according to what they have done in the body, whether good or evil.

Scripture Proofs

1a) Acts 17:31; John 5:27; 1 Cor. 6:3; Jude 6; 2 Peter 2:4; 2 Cor. 5:10; Eccl.12:14; Rom. 2:16, 14:10; Matt. 12:36.

- The end of God's appointing this day is for the manifestation of the glory of His mercy in the eternal salvation of the elect, and of His justice in the damnation of the reprobate who are wicked and disobedient. The righteous shall go into everlasting life and receive that fullness of joy and refreshing which shall come from the presence of the LORD. The wicked, who know not God and obey not the Gospel of Jesus Christ shall be cast into eternal torments and be punished with everlasting destruction from the presence of the LORD and from the glory of His power (Matt.25:31-46; Rom. 2:5, 9:22; Mat. 5:21; Acts 3:19; 2 Thess. 1:7-10).

- As Christ would have us to be certainly persuaded that there shall be a day of judgment both to deter all men from sin, and for the great consolation of the godly in their adversity, so He will have that day unknown to men, that they may shake off all carnal security, and be always watchful because they know not at what hour the LORD will come and may be ever prepared to say, "Come, Lord Jesus, come quickly, Amen." (2 Peter 3:11-14; 2 Cor. 5:10-11; 2 Thess. 1:5-7; Luke 21:7, 28; Rom. 8:23-25; Mat.24:36, 42-44; Mark 13:35-37; Luke 12:35-37; Rev. 22:20)

1689 London Baptist Confession of Faith

Chapter 31

Of the State of Man After Death and of the Resurrection of the Dead

- The bodies of men after death return to dust and see corruption, but their souls which neither die nor sleep, having an immortal substance, immediately return to God who gave them. The souls of the righteous being then made perfect in holiness are received into paradise where they are with Christ and behold the face of God in light and glory, waiting for the full redemption of their bodies. The souls of the wicked are cast into hell where they remain in torment and utter darkness, reserved to the judgment of the great day. Besides these two places, for souls separated from their bodies, the Scriptures acknowledge none (Genesis 3:19; Acts 13:36; Eccl.12:7; 2 Cor. 5:1. 6:8; Phil. 1:23; Heb. 12:23; Jude 6, 7; 1 Peter 3:19; Luke 16:23-24).

- At the last day, such of the saints as are found alive shall not sleep, but be changed, and all the dead shall be raised up with the selfsame bodies and none other, although with different qualities, which shall be united again to their souls forever (1 Cor. 15:42, 43, 51-53; 1 Thess. 4:17; Job 19:26-27).

- The bodies of the unjust shall, by the power of Christ be raised to dishonor. The bodies of the just, by His Spirit unto honor will be made conformable to His own glorious body (Acts 24:15; John 5:28-29; Phil. 3:21).

Chapter 32

Of the Last Judgment

- God has appointed a day wherein He will judge the world in righteousness by Jesus Christ to whom all power is given of the Father. In that day not only will the apostate angels shall be judged, but likewise all persons that have lived upon the earth shall appear before the tribunal of Christ to give an account of their thoughts, words, and deeds, and to receive according to what they have done in the body, whether good or evil (Acts 17:31; John 5:22, 27; 1 Cor. 6:3; Jude 6; 2 Cor. 5:10; Eccl. 12:14; Matt. 12:36; Romans 14;10, 12; Matthew 25:32-46).

- The end of God's appointing this day is for the manifestation of His mercy in the eternal salvation of the elect, and of His justice in the eternal damnation of the reprobate who are wicked and disobedient. The righteous shall go into everlasting life and receive that fulness of joy and glory with everlasting rewards in the presence of the LORD. The wicked who know not God and do not obey the Gospel of Jesus Christ shall be cast aside into everlasting torments and punished with everlasting destruction from the presence of the LORD and from the glory of His power (Romans 9:22-23; Matt. 25:21, 32, 46; 2 Tim. 4:8; Mark 9:48; 2 Thess. 1:7-10).

- As Christ would have us to be certainly persuaded that there shall be a day of judgment, both to deter all men from sin and for the greater consolation of the godly in their adversity, so He will have the day unknown to men, that they may shake off all carnal security, and always be watchful, because they not at what hour the LORD will come. Let us be prepared to say, come, Lord Jesus, come quickly, Amen (2 Cor. 5:10; 2 Thess. 1:5-7; Mark 13:35-37; Luke 12:35-40; Rev. 22:20).

The Baptist Faith and Message (2000 Edition)

© The Southern Baptist Convention

X. Last Things

God, in His own time and His own way, will bring the world to its appropriate end. According to His promise, Jesus Christ will return personally and visibly in glory in the earth. The dead will be raised, and Christ will judge all men in righteousness. The unrighteous will be consigned to hell, the place of everlasting punishment. The righteous in their resurrected and glorified bodies will receive their reward and will dwell forever in heaven with the LORD.

(Isaiah 2:4, 11:9; Matt.16:27, 18:8-9, 19:28, 24:27, 30, 36, 44, 25:31-46; Mark 8:38, 9:43-48; Luke 12: 40, 48, 16:19-26, 17:22-37, 21:17-28; John 14:1-3; Acts 1:11, 17:31; Romans 14:10; 1 Cor. 4:5, 15:24-28, 35-58; 2 Cor. 5:10; Phil. 3:20-21; Col.1:5, 3:4; 1 Th. 4:13-18, 5:1; 2 Th.1:7, 2:1; 1 Tim. 6:14; 2 Tim. 4:1, 8; Titus 2:13; Heb. 9:27-28; James 5:8; 2 Peter 3:7; 1 John 2:28, 3:2; Jude 14; Rev.1:18, 3:10-11; 20:1-22)

A fitting conclusion to this chapter would be to dwell on the promise of Jesus to return one day. All the material, Bible verses, doctrinal statements, history, benefits of study, contributions of godly men in teaching the truths of the Scriptures, and the ever-increasing signs that are coming to pass in our lifetime will come together and be fulfilled on that day when He appears in power and glory. God's people will be at peace, and Israel will worship their Messiah. A new Heaven and Earth is promised to us, and He will be the eternal ruler of the new creation and the paradise that was lost will be restored. None of it would be a reality had Jesus not taken upon Himself the penalty for sin that we deserve, died a horrendous death, and rose from the dead as He proclaimed. When you repent of your sins and surrender your life to Jesus Christ, from that moment on, HE OWNS YOU and expects you to get to know Him through prayer, the study of His Word, sharing your faith, become an active member of a biblically sound church, and to be wary of anyone who presents teachings and sermons that are contrary to Scripture.

Much more information and exposition could have been examined such as the history of the Rapture teaching, the debate over whether or not the United States is part of the prophetic plans of God or not, and if there are real, authentic prophets of God today or not. There are numerous articles, sermons, Bible studies, books, websites, and other material available for you to examine. Just do so with a sense of discretion and careful examination of viewpoints that may not be in line with Scripture.

Men of God such as John MacArthur, David Jeremiah, Adrian Rogers, W.A. Criswell, Dr. Jimmy DeYoung, Billy Crone, J.D. Farag, Charles Stanley, Charles R. Swindoll, John Walvoord, J. Dwight Pentecost, Charles Ryrie, Ed Hindson, Robert Jeffress, R.C. Sproul, Steven Lawson, L.A. Marzulli, Thomas Ice, David Reagan, Randall Price, Donald Grey Barnhouse, James Boice, Ron Rhodes, Don Perkins, Mark Hitchcock, Francis Schaeffer, D. James Kennedy, R.A. Torrey, Martyn Lloyd-Jones, Charles Spurgeon, and Tim LaHaye are all worthy of reading and gaining profound insight not just on prophecy, but other issues that are of spiritual benefit and personal growth. The teachings and sermons of each of these men is solidly grounded in the authority of Scripture and a profound awareness of the holiness and glory of God. Most of them have their own website or have had their work put on one.

Jesus Christ is the foundation on which we rest. That cannot be emphasized enough in this present world with its apparent disregard for the good, pure, holy, and reverent. It was the same way in the time that our LORD walked the earth as a man. The day of the crucifixion stands as a day of apparent darkness and abject cruelty placed upon the One who knew no sin in His life and yet was marching to a hill where He would fulfill His mission. The sorrow of that day was well represented in the 2004 film **The Passion of the Christ**. The scene takes place on what would be known as the Via Delarosa, where the LORD was struggling with each step to carry a huge, heavy cross.

He had nearly been beaten to death and mocked by sadistic Roman guards. His mother was in the back of the crowd watching this spectacle and then sees Him fall to the ground in utter exhaustion and pain. The scene shifts to a time where Jesus is a small boy, playing near his home when He takes a hard fall to the ground. Mary turns to see what had happened, immediately drops everything and runs to Him, picking Him up in her arms and begins to rock Him in her arms, telling Him, "It's all right, I'm here." I remember every woman in the audience begin to shed tears that only a loving, caring mother would do when their little one gets hurt and needs comfort, love, and aid. The scene goes back to the present time, and Mary fights her way through the crowd to get to her Son who is now going to be her Savior. She comes to Him and says the exact words she said to Him when He was little, "It's all right, I'm here, I'm here." She puts her hand on His bleeding face, and He puts His hand on hers, and says, "See, mother…I am making all things new."

Indeed, He has. Glory to God. Amen.

Afterword

It is my prayer that the material which has been presented in this book has been not just a blessing as it pertains to the study of God's Holy Word, but also to give you an overview of the things that are to come in the days ahead according to what God has proclaimed and give you a hunger to know more about His plans to redeem His people, bring justice to the victims of the horrors of sin, to bring judgment upon the wickedness of Satan, his demons, and those who have followed him, and to bring about the eternal rule and reign of the Lord Jesus Christ when He appears again.

The Scriptures tell us to study the Word (Acts 17:11; 2 Timothy 2:15) and to apply it to our lives as we follow Jesus and learn to obey and trust Him in our journey through life and the purposes for which He made us. I ask that you read this book through at least once more, look up the Scripture references, do some research on the historical information that has been presented, look up some of the websites that have been listed and read the writings and viewpoints on scriptural issues that the respective authors and contributors present. Do you agree with their conclusions or not? Know what and why you believe in terms of doctrine and conviction as it pertains to the person and work of the Lord Jesus Christ.

Selected Websites for Biblical and Prophetic Studies

Grace to You, the teaching website of Dr. John MacArthur: www.gty.org

Get A Life Ministries: The website of Bible teacher Billy Crone: www.getalifemedia.com

Ligonier Ministries: Sound Biblical and Doctrinal instruction from a Reformed theological view:

www.ligonier.org

The sermon library of Dr. Adrian Rogers: www.lwf.org

The sermon library of Dr. W.A. Criswell: www.wacriswell.com

Articles on the end times and Biblical studies: www.raptureready.com

Christ in Prophecy: the website of Dr. David Reagan: www.christinprophecy.com

Dr. Martyn Lloyd Jones – outstanding 20th century Welsh preacher: www.mljtrust.org

L.A. Marzulli: Investigations of supernatural events and prophecy: www.lamarzulli.net

Prophecy Watchers television broadcast: www.prophecywatchers.com

Powerful sermons and teaching by Dr. Steven Lawson: www.onepassionministries.com

A collection of messages by great preachers of the past and today: www.sermonaudio.com

I Don't Have Enough Faith to be an Atheist: www.crossexamined.org

Associates for Biblical Research: www.biblearchaeology.org

Dr. Mark Hitchcock, Prophecy Scholar, Author, Pastor: www.markhitchcock.com

A complete library on Bible Topics: www.compellingtruth.org

The website of Dr. John Walvoord (1910-2002) www.walvoord.com

Bibliographic Sources

Chapter 1

- Online data retrieved from the American Federation of Certified Psychics and Mediums, 10 October 2018.

- Online article on "Psychic Hot Lines", accessed 10 October 2018 through www.answers.yahoo.com

- Webster's 1828 Dictionary of the English Language (online). Accessed 11 October 2018.

- "Quotes on Prophecy" accessed through www.brainyqoute.com

- "Quotes on Prophecy" accessed through www.christianquotes.com

- Hitchcock, Mark. The End Carol Stream, IL. Tyndale House, 2014, pp.4-16

- Hester, H.I. The Heart of Hebrew History. Liberty, MO. William Jewell Press, 1949, pp.261-262

- Bullock, C. Hassel. An Introduction to the Old testament Prophetic Books. Chicago, Moody Press, 2007, pp.14-15

Chapter 2

- Bruce, F.F. The Canon of Scripture., Downers Grove, IL. IVP Academic, 1988, pp.216-217.

- McDowell, Josh. More Evidence that Demands A Verdict. Nashville. Thomas Nelson, 1999, pp. 34-40.

- Metzger, Bruce (Gen. Ed.) The Oxford Companion to the Bible. New York, Oxford Press, 1993, p.488.

- Wallace, J. Warner. "Reliability of the New Testament" Article accessed from www.coldcasechristianity.com13 October 2018.

- Roberts, Mark. Blog post accessed from www.patheos.com on October 13, 2018.

- Geisler, Norman (Gen. Ed.) The Popular Handbook of Biblical Archaeology. Eugene, Or., Harvest House, 2013, pp.295-298.

- Webster's 1828 Dictionary (Online). Accessed on October 13, 2018.

- Ibid.

- Pentecost, J. Dwight. Things to Come. Grand Rapids, Academy Books, 1958, pp.14-16

- Walvoord, John. Daniel: A Commentary. Chicago, Moody Press, 2012 (Revised Version), pp.227-228.

- MacDonald, William (Gen. Ed.) Believer's Bible Commentary. Nashville, Thomas Nelson, 1995, p.1084

- Archer, Gleason. "Daniel" in The Expositor's Bible Commentary. Grand Rapids, Zondervan, 1994, pp.1381-1382.

- MacDonald, pp.1227-1228

- Walvoord, John. Matthew: A Commentary. (Revised Edition). Chicago, Moody Press, 2013, pp.97-98.

Chapter 4

- Halley, Henry. Halley's Bible Handbook., Grand Rapids, Zondervan, 1983, pp.285-286.

- Verses in this book marked as NKJV are from The New King James Version of the Holy Bible. © 1982 by Thomas Nelson Publishers, Inc., Nashville, TN.

- Verses in this book marked as NASB are from The Open Bible: New American Standard Version. © The Lockman Foundation, 1960, 1962, 1968, 1971, 1972, 1973, 1975, 1977. A Not-for-Profit Corporation. Bible Study Aids © 1977, 1979 Thomas Nelson, Inc.

(Note to the Reader: The verses from this Edition are to be found in other chapters apart from the information listed here for the sake of convenience.)

Chapter 5

- "Isaiah", an article presented in The Holman Bible Dictionary. Nashville, Holman Publishers, 1991, pp.716-717.

Chapter 6

- MacArthur, John. The MacArthur Bible Commentary. Nashville, Thomas Nelson, 2005, p.932.

- MacDonald, Believer's Bible Commentary. P.1063

Chapter 7

- Pentecost, Things to Come, p.326-328

Chapter 11

- MacArthur, John. The MacArthur New Testament Commentary: John, Chapters. 1-11. Chicago, Moody Press, 2006, p. 9.

- MacArthur, John. Christ's Prophetic Plans. Chicago, Moody Press, 2012, p.208.

- Chafer, Lewis Sperry. Major Bible Themes (2nd Edition). Grand Rapids, Zondervan Publishers, 1974, p.314.

- Hindson, Ed, and LaHaye, Tim. (Gen. Eds.) Popular Encyclopedia of Bible Prophecy. Eugene, OR. Harvest House, 2004, pp.212-213.

- Hindson, Ed, and LaHaye, Tim. (Gen. Eds.) Exploring Bible Prophecy from Genesis to Revelation. Eugene, OR. Harvest House, 2006, p.364.

- Excerpt from an online article on the Rapture written by Dr. David Reagan of Lamb and Lion Ministries. www.christinprophecy.comAccessed May 12, 2020.

- "Expository Notes of Dr. Thomas Constable" accessed from www.studylight.org on May 14, 2020.

- Walvoord, John, and Zuck, Roy B. (Gen. Ed.) The Bible Knowledge Commentary: Volume 2. Wheaton, IL. Victor Books, 1983, p. 322.

- MacArthur, John. The MacArthur New Testament Commentary: John 12-21. Chicago, Moody Press, 2008, pp. 101-102.

Chapter 13

- Hindson and LaHaye, Popular Encyclopedia of Bible Prophecy, p.311

- MacArthur, John. The MacArthur Bible Commentary: 1 Corinthians. Chicago, Moody Press, 1984, p.8 (Introduction)

- Mare, W. Harold. "1 Corinthians" in the Expositor's Bible Commentary. Grand Rapids, Zondervan, 1994, p.654.

- Lowery, David K. "1 Corinthians" in the Bible Knowledge Commentary. Wheaton, IL. Victor Books, 1983, pp.545-546.

- Hindson and LaHaye, Exploring Bible Prophecy from Genesis to Revelation., p.415.

- Walvoord, John. Every Prophecy of the Bible. Colorado Springs, Victor Books, 1999, p. 438.

- McKay, John. Archaeology and the New Testament. Grand Rapids, Baker Books, 2008, pp. 292-293.

- MacArthur, John. The MacArthur New testament Commentary: 1 and 2 Thessalonians. Chicago, Moody Press, 2002, pp.133-137.

- Rhodes, Ron. The End Times in Chronological Order. Eugene, Or. Harvest House, 2012, pp. 50-53.

Chapter 14

- The Westminster Confession of Faith, 1647. Scripture quotes are from the King James Version of the Holy Bible, Public Domain, originally published 1647.

- The 1689 London Baptist Confession of Faith. Scripture quotes are from the King James Version of the Holy Bible, Public Domain.

- The Baptist Faith and Message, 2000 Edition. © The Southern Baptist Convention. Accessed from www.sbc.net on May 26, 2020.

Bibliography of Sources

Online Sources

American Federation of Certified Psychics and Mediums, 2018.

www.brainyquote.com

www.christianquote.com

www.christinprophecy.com

www.coldcasechristianity.com

www.patheos.com

www.studylight.org

Webster's 1828 Online Dictionary of the English Language

Biblical Sources

King James Version of the Holy Bible

New American Standard Bible: Open Bible Edition

New King James Version of the Holy Bible

(All copyright information, dating, and source material has been documented previously.)

Publications

Archer, Gleason. "Daniel" in the Expositor's Bible Commentary. Grand Rapids, Zondervan Publishers, 1994.

Bruce, F.F. The Canon of Scripture. Downers Grove, IL. Grand Rapids, Zondervan Publishers, 1988.

Bullock, C. Hasell. An Introduction to the Old Testament Prophetic Books. Chicago, Moody Press, 2007.

Chafer, Lewis. Major Bible Themes. (2nd Edition). Grand Rapids, Zondervan Publishers, 1974.

Geisler, Norman (Ed.). The Popular Handbook of Biblical Archaeology. Eugene, Or. Harvest House Publishers, 2013.

Halley, Henry H. Halley's Bible Handbook (23rd Edition). Grand Rapids, Zondervan Publishers, 1983.

Hester, H.I. The Heart of Hebrew History. Liberty, MO., William Jewell Press, 1949.

Hindson, Ed. and LaHaye, Tim (Gen. Eds.) Bible Prophecy from Genesis to Revelation. Eugene, OR., Harvest House Publishers, 2006.

_____, Popular Encyclopedia of Bible Prophecy. Eugene, Or., Harvest House Publishers, 2004.

Hitchcock, Mark. The End. Carol Stream, IL., Tyndale House, 2014.

"Isaiah" Holman Bible Dictionary, Nashville, Holman Press, 1991.

Lindsey, David. "1 Corinthians". The Bible Knowledge Commentary. Wheaton, IL., Baker Books, 1983.

MacDonald, William. Believer's Bible Commentary. Nashville, Thomas Nelson, 1995.

Mare, W. Harold. "1 Corinthians", The Expositors Bible Commentary. Grand rapids, Zondervan Publishers, 1994.

MacArthur, John. Christ's Prophetic Plans. Chicago, Moody Press, 2012.

_____ The MacArthur Bible Commentary (One Volume). Nashville, Thomas Nelson, 2005.

_____, The MacArthur Bible Commentary: John, Chapters 1-11; 12-21. Chicago, Moody Press, 2004, 2006.

_____, The MacArthur Bible Commentary: 1 Corinthians. Chicago, Moody Press, 1984.

_____, The MacArthur Bible Commentary: 1 and 2 Thessalonians. Chicago, Moody Press, 2002.

McKay, John. Archaeology and the New Testament. Grand Rapids, Baker Books, 2008.

Metzger, Bruce (Ed.) The Oxford Companion to the Bible. New York, Oxford Press, 1993.

Pentecost, J. Dwight. Things to Come. Grand Rapids, Academy Books, 1958.

Rhodes, Ron. The End Times in Chronological Order. Eugene, OR. Harvest House Publishers, 2012.

Walvoord, John. Daniel: A Commentary. Chicago, Moody Press, 2012.

_____. Every Prophecy of the Bible. Colorado Springs, Victor Books, 1999.

_____. Matthew: A Commentary. Chicago, Moody Press, 2013.

_____, and Zuck, Roy B. (Eds.) The Bible Knowledge Commentary. Wheaton, IL. Victor Books, 1983.

Online Formal Church Confessions and Statements of Belief

The Baptist faith and Message, 2000 Edition. © The Southern Baptist Convention

The 1689 London Baptist Confession of Faith. Public Domain

The Westminster Confession of Faith (1647). Public Domain